# Revival Must Come!

# Revival Must Come!

## By James W. Tharp

A Creation of:

◆◆◆ Christian Renewal
5595 Love Lane
Bozeman, Montana  59715

Published By:
**Companion Press**
**P.O. Box 351**
**Shippensburg, PA 17257-0351**

ISBN 1-56043-478-3

For Worldwide Distribution
Printed in the U.S.A.

# Dedication

To my dear parents, *Jim and Estelle Tharp*, whose paths I followed to Christ in my youth, and whose prayers I feel daily in my ministry. May our Heavenly Father be pleased to grant them even more years of health and strength for their powerful ministry of intercessory prayer. Not until that Great Day will we know the full impact of "the effectual fervent prayers" of these two precious saints.

# Dedication

# Contents

# Contents

# Preface

The eminent British evangelical Martin Lloyd-Jones declared just before his death, "I am profoundly convinced that the greatest need in the world today is revival in the Church of God."

A growing number of Christian leaders agree, yet not all. But those who resent the idea of spiritual awakenings reveal their tragic ignorance of both the history of the Church and of God's purpose for His people.

In 1985, after thirty-six years of pastoral ministry, most of which would have to be described as mediocre, I sensed an urgent direction from the Holy Spirit to curtail much of my professional routine and simply spend time with the Lord. I soon realized that this hunger for God was of God Himself and not just religious fantasy. During the first few weeks of attempted obedience to this new call I was rewarded more than once with unusual manifestations of Christ's Presence. Every special visit deepened the conviction that He was making me a promise: "If you will major in just walking with Me, I will do three things for you: first, I will fill you anew with the Holy Spirit; second, I will teach you to pray; and finally, I will give you a vision of My Church in these last days as I plan to revive it."

For six years now, by the grace of God (and this includes the prayers of many of God's dear children) I have sought earnestly to meet the condition of His promise by giving Him prime time each day. And He has kept His Word, of course.

First, the Lord gave me a new fullness of His Spirit, but not before showing me a cold heart and a slumbering spirit. Following days of Spirit-wrought repentance and brokenness before Him, I received a new cleansing and a new filling and a new freedom.

The new anointing of the Holy spirit brought a new passion and a new empowerment for prayer. What had previously been humanly powered mental exercise now became Spirit-inspired communion and intercession. Little did I realize in early 1986, when all this started to unfold, how far-reaching this new prayer ministry would be. Such praying would of course impact my own congregation, the First Church of the Nazarene in Bozeman, Montana, as key laymen and others desired to attend the prayer seminars to learn the biblical principles of prayer that their pastor was now practicing. And now more doors are opening for the School of Prayer in various denominations and in many cities.

Finally, the Lord has given me a life-changing vision of revival in His Church. In obedience to the leading of the Spirit, *Christian Renewal* was launched, and it is now in its sixth year. This quarterly journal heralds the kind of coming revival that the present generation of Americans has only heard and read about. It sounds the call to Christians in all churches to return to the Upper Room to prepare their hearts and homes and congregations for another full-scale historic spiritual awakening in our land.

I tremble when I think of the only other alternative to revival. But as far gone from righteousness and as ripe for divine judgment as our nation is at this late hour, I share the hope that within the next few years we shall witness the greatest visitation of the Spirit of revival in the history of our country.

Such is the message of this book. *Revival must come!*

# Chapter 1

# The Coming Great Awakening

*O Lord, now I have heard your report, and I worship you in awe for the fearful things you are going to do. In this time of our deep need, begin again to help us, as you did in years gone by. Show us your power to save us. In your wrath, remember mercy.*

Habakkuk 3:2, *The Living Bible*

The strange cycle of the renewal and backsliding of the people of God across the centuries is a haunting phenomenon. The Old Testament Church often failed to meet the conditions of its covenant with Jehovah, and the resulting apostasy wrote tragedy into its history. Christians under the New Covenant are just as guilty of grieving the Spirit of God who lives within them. Such sins are not without serious consequences. The Church does not remain alive unconditionally; it experiences abundant life only as it abides in Christ. "If anyone does not remain in me," warned Jesus, "he is like a branch that is thrown away and withers" (John 15:6).

The prophecy of Habakkuk addresses the mystery and manner in which a holy God deals with His delinquent children. The prophet makes it clear that God will wink at neither the wickedness of the world nor the disobedience of His Church. What He condemns in the world He cannot condone in the Church.

It shocked Habakkuk to learn that it is the prerogative of our sovereign God to choose His method of disciplining His rebellious people. He would use the violence of a plundering Babylon to get the attention of Judah. But the prophet also observed that even in His severe judgments, God is still a God of mercy.

Habakkuk's prayer should inspire our faith in praying for revival today. We should not doubt that God will use the increasing plagues of our time to bring America to repentance. If Charles G. Finney were alive today, he would argue that such awful judgments can actually set the stage for the drama of revival. If Americans will humble themselves and plead moral bankruptcy before a God of holiness and justice, we can yet experience the greatest spiritual awakening in the history of our country.

# Revivals of the Past

God's mighty and merciful acts of reclaiming Israel formed the basis of the prophet's hope that He would do it again. Revival has always been the preserving secret of the people of God. This is so true in the American experience. Three mighty spiritual awakenings have changed the course of our continent on several counts, both sacred and secular.

## The First Awakening

Puritanism, legalism and denominationalism could not hold Colonial America to her spiritual ideals. Long before the end of their first century, the colonies had departed from the old paths. Religious bigotry, austerity and tradition were in great supply, but so were the evils of crime, skepticism, immorality and war—right along with the spiritual backsliding of Christians.

Then, in the late 1720s, the Holy Spirit began preparing a few leaders for an unusual outpouring of new life upon early America. Theodore Frelinghuysen experienced a new anointing as he preached conviction for sin to his startled Dutch Reformed congregation in New Jersey. At almost the same time, Gilbert Tennent and other members of his family were touched by God to light revival fires among the Presbyterians around Philadelphia. Jonathan Edwards, through much prayer and fasting, gave leadership to the Congregational phase of the awakening in New England. Then came George Whitefield to bring the regional revivals together into one mighty movement of the Spirit. The young British evangelist held open-air meetings throughout the Southern and Middle colonies before going up to New England, where the first great awakening demonstrated its greatest power. Whitefield recorded an impression of one of many revival services:

I believe there were near 12,000. I had not spoken long before I perceived numbers melting. As I proceeded, the influence increased till at last, thousands cried out so that they almost drowned my voice...What tears were shed and poured forth after the Lord Jesus...How sweetly did I lie at the feet of Jesus! With what power did a sense of His all-containing love flow in upon my soul![1]

Hundreds of thousands were brought into the kingdom of God in the years between 1720 and 1740. The Church was again able to demonstrate apostolic power and simplicity. The moral and social atmosphere of early America was transformed. The first great awakening shows, said Mendell Taylor, the way a "a rain of righteousness" can reach flood stage and be turned into "a reign of righteousness."[2]

"But the movement subsided like the ebb and flow of the ocean tide," wrote Lewis A. Drummond.[3] Perhaps it was the rising fever of war that choked the revival fires, but all too soon American believers were again trapped in complacency, their cold hearts again in desperate need of the rekindling fires of the Spirit.

## The Second Awakening

God graciously blessed the new republic with another visitation of His reviving power around 1790. The South was included this time, the Methodists and Baptists also playing a major role. The second revival began in Virginia and spread quickly to the Carolinas, then extended to Kentucky, where it gave birth to the camp meeting and produced the colorful circuit-riding preachers who would follow the American frontier with the powerful Gospel so ruggedly and effectively preached by these amazing heroes of the Word.

Men such as James McGready and Barton Stone were leaders in the revival that penetrated the undeveloped communities of Kentucky. They recognized the social and spiritual needs of those living in the sparsely settled wilderness. When they announced prolonged services for those who wished to come with food and camping supplies, people came by the hundreds and then by the thousands, traveling by wagon and horseback and on foot and in canoes.

The Cane Ridge camp meeting in August 1801 attracted 25,000 souls, and from the very first service there was a startling release of divine power. For several days there was no letting up in worship. James B. Finley, a convert in that famous encampment who would become one of the celebrated Methodist circuit riders, wrote of one such service and its impact on his life:

> The noise was like the roar of Niagara. The vast sea of human beings seemed to be agitated as if by a storm...My heart beat tumultuously, my knees trembled, my lips quivered, and I felt as though I must fall to the ground. A strange supernatural power seemed to pervade the entire mass...I stepped up on a log, where I could have a better view of the surging sea of humanity. The scene that presented itself to my mind was indescribable. At one time I saw at least 500 swept down in a moment, as if a battery of a thousand guns had been opened upon them and then immediately followed shrieks and shouts that rent the very heavens.[4]

The second awakening involved other human instruments in places far from the wilderness. Timothy Dwight, President of Yale and grandson of Jonathan Edwards, combined scholarship and evangelistic zeal to confront infidelity in the forms of Rationalism and Deism. One of his first moves as head of Yale was to fire all faculty members caught up in Tom Paine's *The Age of Reason*. He was determined that the Gospel of Jesus Christ would make an impact on the university, and by the year 1802 half of the graduating class had committed their lives to Christ. Undergraduates followed in personal faith, many of whom redirected their lives to the ministry. Yale's spiritual upheaval continued to renew itself long after Dwight's death in 1817.

Lyman Beecher, who loved Timothy Dwight like a father, gave his heart to Christ during his junior year at Yale and became a leader in the second awakening. He also became a patriarch in one of the most influential families in nineteenth-century America. "I was made for action," said Beecher, as he launched a crusade against duelling from his Long Island pulpit, calling it "the national sin." After moving to Litchfield, Connecticut, he gained national prominence by organizing temperance societies to deal with the social evils of alcoholism. Finally, in Boston, Lyman Beecher attacked Unitarianism and experienced the greatest revival of his career.

Francis Asbury was another human factor in the second great awakening. He was commissioned by John Wesley to come to America and head the mission of the Methodist Church. The saddlebag bishop became a legend, covering more territory and being recognized instantly by more people than any other person in the country. Asbury's secret of spiritual power was his daily rising at four in the morning to spend two solid hours in prayer before he began attending to other matters. He knew the source of the revivals in his own ministry and he did not hesitate to call his preachers to the discipline of prayer and fasting.

The important duty of fasting has become almost obsolete. This we are afraid will be productive of melancholy effects. We yet have abundant cause for deep humiliation before God and one another. Our country is threatened, calamities stare us in the face, iniquity abounds, and the love of many waxes cold. O let us again resort to fasting and humiliation.[5]

The second awakening met with the same dying end as the first. In a combination of distractions, the revival fires burned out in the middle of the second decade of the nineteenth century.

## The Third Awakening

Around 1820, the country again experienced phenomenal outbursts of divine power and a third movement of the Spirit was launched. Lewis Drummond considered this awakening to have lasted for about thirty years—from the time of the conversion of Charles G. Finney to the great laymen's prayer revival of 1858-60, which launched the ministry of D. L. Moody.[6]

Throughout more than three decades of high spiritual tide, practically all of the Northeast was touched. Under Finney, entire cities turned to God. What happened in the churches penetrated the moral and social fabric of communities as a new God-consciousness gripped the country.

But once more the revival fires ceased to burn as the passions and politics of the Civil War plagued the land.

On several occasions and in many places on our continent between 1895 and 1905 there were hopeful signs of another unusual awakening. Again, following World War II, there were spiritual tremors in over a dozen places. In the 1950s and 1970s, reports of glorious outbreaks came from Kentucky, Indiana, Illinois and the Canadian provinces of Alberta and Manitoba. But the sad truth is that not since the beginning of the Civil War has the North American continent known the

kind of rending of the heavens that seizes the minds and
hearts of the masses and restores the fear of God to the land.

*I believe it is going to happen again!*

# The Crying Need Today

God listened as His prophet cried, "In this time of our
deep need, begin again to help us, as you did in years gone
by." But it is not just preachers who are calling for a moral
and spiritual awakening in our land. A university professor,
when asked by Billy Graham what he considered to be the
greatest need in our country today, replied:

> I may surprise you, because I'm not a religious person, but I
> believe that the greatest need we have at this hour is a
> spiritual awakening which will restore individual and collec-
> tive morals and integrity throughout the nation.[7]

The apostle Paul wrote about a messed-up civilization so
totally insensitive to God's grace that it was given over to a
downward spiral of perversion (Rom. 1:18-32). When a
generation arrogantly closes its mind to the evidence of God,
Paul argued, it sinks deeper and deeper into the swamps of its
own sick behavior. Those who reject divine revelation are
soon able to ignore conscience, and those who ignore conscience will in time refuse to listen to reason. America is rapid-
ly approaching this dreadful point of moral insanity. Only a
mighty, merciful act of God can save us.

**Read and Weep**

● *Broken Home and Lives*—The tragedy of divorce
breaks the hearts of at least four million women, children and

men in our country every year. Only the victims themselves can grasp the meaning of family breakup in terms of human suffering—rejection, guilt, remorse, bitterness, loss of self-esteem, loneliness, fear and financial hardship. Oh, for a visitation of the divine Physician Who alone can heal our broken hearts and wounded spirits!

● *A Sexual Wilderness*—That our nation has so brazenly violated the sacred gift of sex is proved by our adultery, illegitimacy, perversity, pornography and vulgarity. Adultery is glamorized by television, film industries and the printed page. Pornography has grown into a multi-billion-dollar business that feeds on sickened minds and diseased wills enslaved by lust, violence and sadomasochism. Homosexuals are gaining in their fight for a respected gay society. Even the horrible disease of AIDS, which threatens the whole population, is not considered by this pleasure-bent generation to be any kind of warning by God or nature against the evil of sexual perversion.

Only one hope remains: the kind of revival that measures high enough on God's Richter scale to storm the gates of hell and send demonic captors fleeing in terror before the crashing waves of divine enlightenment, bringing the captives of sin to an awful realization of their horrible state, granting them a spirit of repentance and restoring moral sanity and decency, and mercifully opening the gates of the Kingdom in a mighty deliverance for all who will call upon the name of the Lord.

● *Abortion, Crime, Drugs and Violence*—How must the Creator feel about a nation that crusades to save birds and animals while it kills millions of its unborn babies? What kind of prison reform will it take to remedy our national disgrace of overflowing jails and prisons? Law-enforcement agencies have almost given up on the omnipresent drug traffic, as millions destroy their brains and nerves with dope. Crimes of violence are so common that millions in our cities live in a state of fear day and night.

If the antediluvian world broke the heart of God as He "saw that the wickedness of man was great in the earth, and that every imagination of the thoughts of his heart was only evil continually" (Gen. 6:5, *RSV*), what is His disposition towards America at this dark hour?

Christians must follow Habakkuk's daring course and seek a merciful move on the part of Almighty God. If He can find the Noahs in our land who will set their houses in order and intercede for a world that deserves wrath, I believe there will be a reprieve during which our nation once more will be shaken to its depths in revival. As long as the Noahs prevail with God, the flood of destruction will be withheld. Let Christian leaders call for seasons of repentance and intercessory prayer. We must not sit around and wait for God's wrath; we must fall to our knees and beg for mercy.

● *A Spirit of Lying*—A free society depends on a code of honor that cherishes the truth. But the American public is more cynical today about the integrity of its leadership and institutions than at any time since the Watergate scandal. The apostle could have been speaking of our society when he wrote, "Their throats are open graves; their tongues practice deceit. The poison of vipers is on their lips. Their mouths are full of cursing and bitterness" (Rom. 3:13-14). Politicians lie to get elected. Scientists falsify research to get attention and grants. Merchants lie in their advertising to outsell competitors. Attorneys lie to the jury to save their clients. Millions cheat on their income tax reports to save money. The alarming decline in basic honesty now threatens the whole fabric of the American society . It will require an extraordinary visitation of the God of truth to deal with human treachery and hypocrisy. One sign that a God of holiness is again moving through the land in revival will be the wail that becomes a national chorus: "Woe is me! for I am undone; because I am a man of unclean lips, and I dwell in the midst of a people of unclean lips" (Isa. 6:5, *KJV*).

# It's Now or Never

I realize that many Christians expect nothing more at this late hour except the wrath of God to be poured out on wicked America, just as it was on Noah's generation and just as it was visited on Sodom and Gomorrah. This surely is what we deserve. But as difficult as it is for us to accept, it is not our pagan society in its appalling moral darkness that prevents the mighty revival so desperately needed. It is the sleeping majority in the Church that is responsible for the spiritual famine in the land.

### "Repent or Else!"

Five of the seven churches addressed by the Lord in the book of Revelation were commanded to repent. That same call is going out to the slumbering body of Christ at this hour. May we have an ear to hear what the Spirit is saying to the churches! If Christian leaders knew what is about to come to pass on the face of the earth they would immediately proclaim special seasons of prayer and repentance for themselves and for the Church and for the world. "We can wear out our knees praying for revival," wrote Peter Marshall and David Manuel, "but if we are not willing to go through the pain of repentance, the Great Awakening we seek will not come."[8]

The Spirit is calling the Church to repent of sin—coldness of heart, self-righteousness, a slumbering spirit, prayerlessness, slothful stewardship, substitutions for spiritual life, a carnal pride that refuses to humble itself. Even as the world staggers toward the edge of the precipice, God calls His people out of their sleep to prepare the way for revival: *"If my people, who are called by my name, will humble themselves and pray and seek my face and turn from their wicked ways, then I will hear from heaven and will forgive their sin and will heal their land"* (II Cron. 7:14).

## Holy Violence Needed

"From the days of John the Baptist until now," Jesus challenged us, "the kingdom of heaven has been forcefully advancing, and forceful men lay hold of it" (Matt. 11:12). Kingdom business, and revival in particular, requires men and women with a holy boldness to take hold of the purposes of God and move forward to tear down Satanic strongholds. This kind of holy violence is what E. M. Bounds called for when the revival fires had gone out in nineteenth-century America:

> No amount of money, genius, or culture can move things for God. Holiness energizes the soul, the whole man aflame with love, with desire for more faith, more prayer, more zeal, more consecration—this is the secret of power. These we need and must have, and men must be the incarnation of this God-inflamed devotedness. God's advance has been

stayed, His cause crippled, His name dishonored for their lack. Genius (though the loftiest and most gifted), education (though the most learned and refined), position, dignity, place, honored names, high ecclesiastics cannot move this chariot of our God. It is a fiery one, and fiery forces only can move it. The genius of a Milton fails. The imperial strength of a Leo fails. Brainerd's spirit can move it. Brainerd's spirit was on fire for God, on fire for souls. Nothing earthly, worldly, selfish came in to abate in the least the intensity of this all-impelling and all-consuming force and flame.[9]

Every revival since Pentecost has begun in the Upper Room. God is calling us back to the place of prayer for repentance and brokenness, for cleansing and filling of His Spirit, for faith and vision in the reviving of His Church. Only then can we with pure hearts and clean hands prevail in prayer for the supernatural awakening He wants to give. Samuel Chadwick wrote:

There is no power like that of prevailing prayer—of Abraham pleading for Sodom, Jacob wrestling in the stillness of the night, Moses standing in the breach, Hannah intoxicated with sorrow, David heartbroken with remorse and grief, Jesus in sweat and blood...Such prayer prevails. It turns ordinary souls into men of power...It brings fire. It brings rain. It brings life. It brings God.[10]

## Time is Running Out

The hour is late. The people of God must make up their minds about their commitment to the only hope for a mighty awakening—that of prevailing prayer. We must pray with the prophet, *"Oh, that you would tear the heavens open and come down—at your Presence the mountains would melt*

*as fire sets brushwood alight, as fire causes water to boil—*
*to make known your name to your enemies, and make the*
*nations tremble at your Presence, working unexpected*
*miracles such as no one has ever heard of before"* (Isa.
64:1-3, *The Jerusalem Bible*).

May the glory of God burst on the American Church with
such power that we will sing with Charles Wesley:

> See how great a flame aspires,
> Kindled by a spark of grace!
> Jesu's love the nation fires,
> Sets the kingdoms on a blaze.
> To bring fire on earth He came;
> Kindled in some hearts it is:
> O that all might catch the flame,
> All partake the glorious bliss.
>
> When He first the work begun,
> Small and feeble was His day:
> Now the word doth swiftly run,
> Now it winds its widening way;
> More and more it spreads and grows
> Ever mighty to prevail;
> Sin's strongholds it now o'erthrows,
> Shakes the trembling gates of hell.
>
> Sons of God, your Savior praise!
> He the door hath opened wide;
> He hath given the word of grace,
> Jesu's word is glorified;
> Jesu, mighty to redeem,
> He alone the work hath wrought;

Worthy is the work of Him,
Him who spake a world from nought.

Saw ye not the cloud arise,
Little as a human hand?
Now it spreads along the skies,
Hangs o'er all the thirsty land;
Lo! the promise of a shower
Drops already from above;
But the Lord will shortly pour
All the Spirit of His love![11]

# Notes

1. George Whitefield, *Journals* (Billings & Sons, 1960), p. 425.

2. Mendell Taylor, *Exploring Evangelism* (Beacon Hill, 1964). p. 404.

3. Lewis A. Drummond, *The Awakening that Must Come* (Broadman, 1978), pp. 14-15.

4. James B. Finley, *Autobiography* (Methodist Book Concern, 1853), pp. 166-167.

5. L. D. Rudolph, *Francis Asbury* (Abingdon, 1966), p. 143.

6. Drummond, *Op. Cit.*, pp. 17-18.

7. Billy Graham, "Needed: A Heaven-sent Revival," *Decision*, Vol.28, No. 2, pp. 1-2.

8. Peter Marshall and David Manuel, *From Sea to Shining Sea* (Fleming H. Revell, 1986), p. 406.

9. E. M. Bounds, *Power through Prayer* (Zondervan, 1962), p. 46.

10. Samuel Chadwick, quoted by Leonard Ravenhill, *Revival Praying* (Bethany Fellowship, 1962), p. 44.

11. Charles Wesley, *The Methodist Hymn Book* (Methodist Conference Office, 1933), No. 263.

# Chapter 2

# Preparing the Way

*Prepare the way for the Lord,*
*make straight paths for him.*
*Every valley shall be filled in,*
*every mountain and hill made low.*
*The crooked roads shall become straight,*
*the rough ways smooth.*
*And all mankind will see God's salvation.*

Luke 3:4-6

Revival is the marvelous work of our Sovereign God, but He begins it by preparing the hearts of His people for repentance and obedience. Revival is a new beginning of obedience to God's Word.

John the Baptist was sent by God to prepare Israel for the coming of her Messiah. As the forerunner of Christ, John quoted Isaiah to show the urgency of preparing the way. Preparation meant repentance, and the Baptist spelled out its meaning: *to straighten up one's heart and life in line with God's Word.*

In ancient times the city fathers would send a delegation to the royal court to petition the king to honor their city with a visit. But the king would send a forerunner to that city to test the sincerity of the invitation. Did the people realize the significance of a royal visit? Were they aware of all the necessary preparations? Would they be willing to build the kind of road over which the royal chariot could roll—filling in depressions, leveling high places, straightening sharp curves and smoothing out the rough places? The king would be delighted to visit the city, but there was more to the visitation than a mere invitation.

Revival talk is cheap, but genuine revival preparation is costly. This writer has been in revival work long enough to know that only a fraction of the churches sending out invitations are willing to prepare for the coming of the Lord in a special revival visitation. Charles G. Finney once observed that if farmers planned for their crops the way churches prepared for revival, the whole world would have starved long ago.

John's message to Israel to prepare for her King has special meaning for the Church today.

## Filling in the Valleys

"Every valley shall be filled in," demanded the prophet. Valleys represent the breaks, divisions and depressions in the earth's surface. God's messengers used them to illustrate the inner defeats in the lives of the people. Since the New Testament fairly rings with the promise of fullness and power, Christians must take responsibility for their inner emptiness and defeat. Joyless saints must face their spiritual vacuum and own their needs before new life in the Spirit can come.

## The Valley of Disobedience

Jesus associated obedience and joy in a cause-and-effect relationship. "If you obey my commands," He told His disciples, "you will remain in my love, just as I have obeyed my Father's commands and remain in his love. I have told you this so that my joy may be in you and that your joy may be complete" (John 15:10-11). Christians who continue day after day with little or no joy must examine their hearts for possible disobedience.

What is going on in your life that God cannot bless? What command might you be overlooking? Take your Bible and turn to Psalm 139:23-24: "Search me, O God, and know my heart; test me and know my anxious thoughts. See if there is any offensive way in me, and lead me in the way everlasting." I promise that if you really want to know what has robbed you of your joy, just pray this prayer and stay tuned to the Spirit. He will show you what is necessary to restore the joy of your salvation.

Ezekiel was cautioned by the Lord against being taken in by those who appeared excited with his messages (Ezek. 33:30-32). There were strange motives in the hearts of his listeners. The prophet was to them an entertainer. The people went away unchanged and impenitent. Church members today may speak highly of their pastors and invite others to their churches while not obeying the Word that is preached. Jesus asked, "Why do you call me, 'Lord, Lord,' and do not do what I say?" (Luke 6:46). Disobedience will lock up the heavens and dry up the soul. But repentance and obedience will bring the joy of the Lord.

## The Quicksands of Doubt

Disobedience and doubt are twin evils that must be dealt with before revival can come. Dietrich Bonhoeffer wrote:

No one should be surprised at the difficulty of faith if there is some part of his life where he is consciously resisting or disobeying the commandment of Jesus. Is there some part of your life which you are refusing to surrender at his behest, some sinful passion, maybe, or some animosity, some hope, perhaps your ambition or your reason? If so, you must not be surprised that you have not received the Holy Spirit, that prayer is difficult, or that your request for faith remains un-answered. Go rather and be reconciled with your brother; renounce the sin which holds you fast—and then you will recover your faith! If you dismiss the word of God's com-mand, you will not receive the word of his grace. How can you hope to enter into communion with him when at some point in your life you are running away from him? The man who disobeys cannot believe, for only he who obeys can believe.[1]

One of the fruits of doubt is anxiety, and this is primarily a spiritual problem. Doubting Christians are not trusting every-thing to the Lord, so they worry and fret. Anxiety in the human spirit should signal us that the work of the Holy Spirit is being hindered. When we fret over failure, danger or the fu-ture, negative forces move in to control and prevent the work of God in us. To know a fresh visitation of the Spirit for clear-ing away such darkness, we must confess our doubts and anxieties and accept God's forgiveness and cleansing.

## The Dungeon of Depression

"Why are you downcast, O my soul? Why so disturbed within me?" the depressed psalmist asked himself (Ps. 42:5).

When unhappy Christians are as determined to get at the bottom of their problem as was the psalmist, they will find some answers. What is the source of this loss of hope that sucks from us our energy and enthusiasm for worship and the work of the Lord? This preoccupation with our hurts and needs is a disease of selfishness that undercuts our faith and ability to tap into resurrection power for divine deliverance. As we confess and repent of this spiritual failure, God will open the doors of our emotional prison and we can sing with Wesley:

> Long my imprisoned spirit lay,
>     Fast bound in sin and nature's night.
> Thine eyes diffused a quick'ning ray.
>     I woke; the dungeon flamed with light.
> My chains fell off; my heart was free.
>     I rose, went forth, and followed Thee.[2]

# Leveling the Mountains

"Every valley shall be filled in, every mountain and hill made low" said the prophet. When the children of Israel entered Canaan, they discovered that the pagan inhabitants had erected altars and temples on their mountains and higher elevations. There they worshiped their many gods. Jehovah ordered His people to completely conquer the pagan tribes, and this included the destruction of their false system of worship (Deut. 12:2-3). When Israel failed to destroy these high places of idolatry, the places actually became a snare to her, and she sought at times to offer there a strange mixture of worship herself. Such worship was of course completely unacceptable to Jehovah.

## Hedonism in High Places

Showing how the Israelites lost the Promised Land through self-indulgence, Paul warned Christians against the idolatry of pleasure (I Cor. 10:1-14). "Do not be idolaters, as some of them were; as it is written: 'The people sat down to eat and drink and got up to indulge in pagan revelry.' " Only six weeks after making their covenant with Jehovah, the children of Israel found nothing more important to do than eat and drink and dance before the golden calf. There was nothing to distinguish them from the pagan world except their past, which they had sadly forgotten. So Paul flashed a warning to all of us lest we too turn aside from our first love to Christ and succumb to the appeal of the sensual. In losing control of our appetites we fall into slavery of the most dreaded taskmasters. The true measure of one's bondage to food and drink can be taken only at the time of the Spirit's call to a deeper devotion to Christ through prayer and fasting. All too many cannot even hear the call. Thousands cannot abstain from food for even a short season, and the reasons are not all medical. The worst thing about overindulgent Christians is not their personal appearance or even their tendency towards hypertension and heart ailments, but their loss of appetite for the things of God.

Only the weapons of an Elijah can come against the gods of pleasure today. Elijah was no superman, but a normal human being, said the apostle James (5:17). He was weak, subject to doubts, fears and depression. Then how could he confront wicked Ahab and idolatrous Jezebel? How could he call a contest with the prophets of Baal and witness a confirming flash of celestial fire on the altars of Mount Carmel? From the account of his life in I Kings we suspect that the prophet had not always known how to mobilize divine power to tear down the strongholds of evil. James revealed the humiliating process through which Elijah endured: confession, prayer, healing and suffering (James 5:16-18). With his heart cleansed and his spirit whole, Elijah prayed the effectual, fervent prayer. Such spiritual warfare could "demolish arguments and every pretension that sets itself up against the knowledge of God" (II Cor. 10:5).

Many professing Christians have been taken captive by their fleshly desires. Some are so tormented by demonic forces that they are unable to control their thoughts. Others are compulsive eaters, having given up all hopes of any dieting measures. Too many, including pastors, are addicted to cable and network television programming, no longer shocked by the sounds of profanity or the scenes of adultery.

The Church need not sit powerless against such bondage. The Spirit is calling out men and women who will allow their hearts to be stirred to pray *earnestly*. As Jesus said "This kind can come out only by prayer" (Mark 9:29).

## Altars of Self-worship.

The philosophy of self-fulfillment still prevails throughout most of the Western world. Referring particularly to the American attempt to make self sovereign, Christopher Lasch spoke of "the narcissistic preoccupation with self."[3]

Charles Colson confronted the Church for its failure to provide the light for those lost in self-obsession:

> ...the church is in almost as much trouble as the culture,
> for the church has bought into the same value system:
> fame, success, materialism, celebrity. We watch the leading

churches and the leading Christians for our cues. We want to emulate the best-known preachers with the biggest sanctuaries and the grandest edifices.

Preoccupation with these values has also perverted the church's message. The assistant to one renowned media pastor, when asked the key to his man's success, replied without hesitation, "We give the people what they want." This heresy is at the root of the most dangerous message preached today: the what's-in-it-for-me gospel.[4]

God has made His own provision for our fulfillment, but it is not one that overlooks our sinful nature. He draws us to Christ to share both His death and His resurrection. God's primary purpose for us is not the pursuit of pleasure, happiness, achievement or success; He has saved us "to be conformed to the likeness of His Son" (Rom. 8:29). Strangely enough, this process of fulfillment is one of self-denial, not self-gratification.

A God of holiness will keep His distance from a people caught up in the false religion of self-worship. But when they are sickened of their idolatry, when they have torn down their high places, and when they have returned to the one true altar containing the only sacrifice acceptable to God, the fire will again fall from heaven in cleansing and reviving power.

# Straightening the Crooked Roads

A God of moral purity will not walk a crooked path with anyone, no matter how religious he may claim to be. "The crooked roads shall become straight." If revival is a new beginning in honesty with God, then it is high time we begin to straighten our walk.

## Treachery

"The heart is deceitful above all things, and beyond cure. Who can understand it?" (Jer. 17:9). The prophet answered in the very next verse: "I the *Lord* search the heart and examine the mind."

In presenting a radical remedy for sin, Jesus read the ugly x-rays of the uncleansed human heart to His disciples: "For from within, out of men's hearts, come evil thoughts, sexual immorality, theft, murder, adultery, greed, malice, deceit, lewdness, envy, slander, arrogance and folly" (Mark 7:21-22). One of the thirteen characteristics of the defiled heart mentioned here is *deceit* (scheming, trickery, luring, snaring, treachery).

Two important men in the Bible—Jacob, an Old Testament patriarch, and Judas, one of Christ's disciples—reveal the defiling fruits of a treacherous heart. In the first we learn of a radical remedy, while in the last we behold the final tragedy.

Jacob deceived his father and stole his brother's birthright. He went on to scheme his way to prosperity until at last God hemmed him in with trouble on all sides. Only then did Jacob turn to God in complete surrender. All night he wrestled with God—God wrested from him a confession of his despicable nature and Jacob wrested from God a promise that He would bless him. In the course of the struggle, "Jacob's thigh was put out of joint" (Gen. 32:25, *RSV*). The flesh was marked with weakness in order that Jacob might thereafter walk in the power of God. In a night of repentance he exchanged self-sufficiency for divine enablement, the name of Jacob for the name of Israel, and a life of the bitter fruits of the flesh for a new day of power with God and with men.

Judas, on the other hand, being warned by our Lord of his treachery, went right on stonewalling to his tragic end. He chose to excuse, rationalize or justify his traitorous action rather than come out into the light with Christ and confess his devious nature.

Christians, we have got to be willing to take the lid off our lives and completely expose ourselves before the God of light. Whatever He reveals as belonging to darkness must be confessed and purged if we are to continue to live as His children. Only this kind of openness before the Lord will save us from the Judas spirit of treachery. Honesty before the Lord, transparency in home and church relationships and an openness before the world will prepare the way for revival.

## Hypocrisy

If we believe that divine worship is the highest purpose and noblest act of man, we should see to it that every part is free from pretense. Inability and unwillingness to worship fully and freely in the power of the Spirit is the very point at which revival is hindered in many churches.

Jesus confronted the hypocrisy of the Pharisees with a quote from Isaiah: "These people honor me with their lips, but their hearts are far from me. They worship me in vain; their teachings are but rules taught by men" (Mark 7:6-7). John R. W. Stott commented:

> They were not true worshippers at all, but play actors. The honor they gave to God was pretense, not reality. And the essential distinction here is between the worship of the lips and the heart.[5]

The fraudulent worship of the Pharisees is so serious that only a few ever hear the call to repentance. Before any kind of religious experience worthy of the name of revival can sweep our North American churches, there must first come a genuine sense of remorse for our shameful travesty of divine worship. Concerning this awful sham, we must rend our hearts as well as our garments.

## Dishonesty

The early Church was beautiful in its purity and power and simplicity of worship. Then came Ananias and Sapphira. They envied those who were blessed by God, who were held in esteem by men for their generous giving. The crafty pair devised a scheme whereby they thought they might win the same respect as Barnabas and others and still hold on to a part of what they would claim had been given. They sold a property and gave a part of the price to the apostles to be used for the poor. The amount of money given was incidental; their conspiracy to pretend before God and their fellow Christians that they were giving all was fatal. Their dishonesty was immediately challenged by the Holy Spirit, who revealed their hypocrisy to Peter. "How is it that you have contrived this deed in your heart?" the apostle asked. "You have not lied to men but to God," he announced (Acts 5:4, *RSV*). Ananias had a fatal seizure on the spot, to be followed by his wife three hours later.

Those who knowingly testify to a false devotion to God are seldom stricken with instant physical death, but their spiritual death is swift. Deception and cover-up bring tragedy in the Church, but brokenness and confession clear the way for revival. When we see professing Christians straightening up their crooked paths, we know that the Holy Spirit is preparing the Church for an unusual awakening.

# Smoothing the Rough Ways

Some who may not have deep valleys to fill in or high mountains to level or crooked paths to straighten up may have some dislocated areas of their lives that need to be brought into alignment with God's Word. Relationships can go awry and hinder fellowship. The human spirit can get infected and break forth in looseness of tongue—rash judgment, a bit of gossip, an unwise statement. Christians sometimes give in to the flesh by allowing themselves to get mentally and spiritually lazy. Or for some unexplained reason they can withhold devotion and service to the Lord. Such unattended rough places will put us on a spiritual decline. Such neglect has consequences. All too soon we drop below the spiritual poverty level.

All who have received the gift of eternal life should remember Christ's promise of *abundant* life (John 10:10). All true followers of Christ have everlasting life, but too few of them have it to the full. All have the Holy Spirit, but not many are filled with the Spirit. We must in these days pray for an awakening that will bring us back to the fullness of the Holy Spirit. Church members trapped in nominalism, legalism and indifference must be set free. God's children are wounded, discouraged, empty, confused and ready to quit. They must rediscover the Balm in Gilead.

Such powerful healing will come to the Church and to our land again only as we prepare the way.

# Notes

1. Dietrich Bonhoeffer, *The Cost of Discipleship* (Mac-Millan Pub. Co., 1961), pp. 72-73.

2. Charles Wesley, "And Can It Be?" *Worship in Song* Lillenas Pub. Co., 1972), No. 221.

3. Christopher Lasch, *The Culture of Narcissism: American Life in an Age of Diminishing Expectations* (Warner Books, 1979).

4. Charles Colson, *Loving God* (Zondervan, 1983). p. 14.

5. John R. W. Stott, *Christ the Controversialist* (Inter-Varsity, 1978), p. 161.

# Chapter 3

# "To the Seven Churches"

*To the seven churches in the province of Asia:*

*Grace and peace to you from him who is, and who was, and who is to come, and from the seven spirits before his throne, and from Jesus Christ, who is the faithful witness, the firstborn from the dead, and the ruler of the kings of the earth.*

*To him who loves us and has freed us from our sins by his blood, and has made us to be a kingdom and priests to serve his God and Father—to him be glory and power for ever and ever! Amen.*

Revelation 1:4-6

Blessed is the Christian who knows the book of Revelation to be more than doomsday talk, and who doesn't whine about the frightening imagery of the last book in his New Testament. Blessed is the intelligent reader who understands what apocalyptic literature meant to the original readers, who accepts the vision as firmly rooted in history and proclaiming

Christ as Lord of the past, the present and the future. Blessed is the believer who will allow neither brilliant skeptic nor fanatical speculator to keep his mind and heart from the urgent message of the book of Revelation.

## Seven Representative Churches

The glorified Shepherd appeared to His beloved apostle to give him a message for His straying flock. He addressed seven local churches in the Roman province that is now Western Turkey.

In a book whose numbers are highly significant, the choice of seven (symbolic of completeness) would assure the readers that this message was intended for the whole Church throughout its entire age. And the choice of these particular seven assemblies was no doubt made on the basis of their accurate representation of all the virtues and vices of the historic Church through the centuries.

## Three Great Perils

Dangers from both within and without the Church threatened the followers of Christ at the time of the vision.

● *Persecution*—While Nero was the first emperor to move violently against Christians, his persecution was sporadic and confined mostly to Rome. Now—twenty-five years later, at the time of John's exile—Domitian was moving fiercely against believers in the Roman province of Asia. They were often boycotted in business. Some were prevented from buying and selling because they refused to burn incense before the image of the emperor. More than a few were killed for their loyalty to Christ.

● *Heresy*—Doctrinal error was rampant as false teachers feverishly worked the churches like an army of insects trying to devour the crops ahead of the harvest. Their strange philosophies and seducing doctrines appealed to pride and lust and greed. The results were tragic: confusion, division and despair.

● *Sin*—Disobedience to the Word took its toll in the forms of idolatry, immorality and apathy. The risen Lord appeared to John to assure the Church that He ever lived to comfort those who suffered for Him, to correct those who strayed from Him and to command repentance of all who disobeyed Him.

# A Revelation of Christ

John reported from a barren Aegean island that he worshiped "in the Spirit" (Rev. 1:10). Perhaps he meant that he was caught up in a state of rapture, but the intent of his testimony is to attribute what he saw and heard of the glorified Christ to the work of the Spirit.

## A Renewing Vision

John knew that not all was well with his fellow Christians on the mainland, and in his captivity this added to his burden of daily intercessory prayer. As far as he knew, he was the only surviving apostle. His brother James had been slain by Herod. Peter had been crucified. Paul had been beheaded in Rome. All the rest had disappeared, with rumors circulating of their violent deaths. John's mind went back more than sixty years to the times when they had been together with the Master. Perhaps he was swept by a longing to hear that stately voice again, to see that face of splendor once more, to feel

His transforming touch. Suddenly, John was hearing a loud voice behind him. He turned to see...

*Someone "like a son of man."* The very One John had known in years past stood before him in His glorified humanity.

*Dressed in a robe reaching down to his feet and with a golden sash around his chest.* This was not the seamless robe of yesterday, but the uniform of the Great High Priest who was in the business of offering atonement for a wayward Church.

*His head and hair were white like wool, as white as snow.* Using Daniel's language to describe the "Ancient of Days" (Dan. 7:9), John caught something of the transcending holiness and wisdom of the Mighty One.

*His eyes were like blazing fire.* Here was the scrutiny of omniscience; He would never be deceived by anyone. All would be open to His gaze.

*His feet were like bronze glowing in a furnace.* This Great High Priest was also the final Judge of all. He had become a consuming fire.

*His voice was like the sound of rushing waters.* Like the roar of a thousand Niagaras, His voice will silence all others.

*In his right hand he held seven stars.* The right hand being the symbol of power, the churches and their ministers could never live and shine unless they were under the control of this Sovereign One.

*Out of his mouth came a sharp double-edge sword.* The sword represents conquest, but this Conqueror's power is spoken; it is the very Word of God!

*His face was like the sun shining in all its brilliance.* Reminded of the Transfiguration, John saw in the countenance of the glorified Lord the hope of the Church and of the entire human race.

## A Reviving Voice

Such a vision was so overpowering that John reacted as had Joshua, Ezekiel and Daniel—he fell before the Lord as if he were a dead man.

"Do not be afraid," Christ said, and He reached down to touch His favorite disciple now grown old and weak. The blinding splendor subsided for a moment as John recognized the face and voice he had longed for. His touch revived him, but that marvelous voice was speaking, and John had to listen...

*I am the First and the Last.* Here in Person was the Absolute Creator and Lord of history.

*I am the Living One; I was dead, and behold I am alive for ever and ever!* He's the very One John remembered, the One who through His death and resurrection had become Head of the Church. Now He lived to call His followers and the whole world to account.

*And I hold the keys of death and Hades.* His authority extends over the realm of death; He makes the regions of Hades serve His aims.

John soon understood the urgency of such a startling vision for the floundering churches—it was their only answer. He wrote diligently, knowing that his message straight from the glorified Christ would mean revival.

The revival so desperately needed by the American churches today can come only by a new revelation of the glory of Christ. And this is the special work of the Holy Spirit.

◆◆◆

# An Examination of the Church

John saw *seven golden lampstands* with Christ in their midst. He did not see a single candelabra with seven branches, but seven separate lampstands. Christ was walking among them, inspecting each one. He deals with each church and individual. He walks among us today—commending, confronting and commanding repentance. He brings with Him the blood of atonement and the oil of anointing.

## What Christ Commended

● *Aglow in the Spirit*—Even among such indifferent and lukewarm churches as Ephesus, Sardis and Laodicea, Christ found those who were fervently devoted to Him. A divine visitation to a cold church will be prompted by God's grace in response to the prevailing prayers of those who "pray the price" to maintain the glory of God on their lives and churches.

● *Zealous of Good Works*—Every church is examined for works of righteousness. This is sometimes surprising to evangelicals, since we emphasize salvation by grace. But looking at one of our classic texts of salvation (Eph. 2:8-10) we see the proper formula: it is by *grace* through *faith* unto *good works*. Do we realize that all who are saved by grace through faith must be judged by their works? (Rom. 14:9-12; I Cor. 3:12-15; II Cor. 5:10).

● *Sound Doctrine*—The Lord measured all the churches and their leaders for their accuracy in holding carefully to His plain and simple teachings. Even cold-hearted Ephesus was commended for her ability to discern the designs of false teachers.

● *Suffering Saints*—The Savior was tenderly drawn to Smyrna in her suffering for His name. The attention and comfort given her should remind us that He knows every hardship we endure, every reproach we suffer and every bit of energy we expend for His sake.

● *Abiding Faith*—Smyrna's faith had been purified through suffering. Even among Pergamum and Sardis were those who had not denied the faith. There is a special place in the heart of Christ for all who trust and obey Him at the risk of everything. But He warned that this kind of faith would be scarce in the last days (Luke 18:8).

## What Christ Confronted

● *Coldness of Heart*—Ephesus had forsaken its first love. The spirit of Sardis was dead. The devotion of Laodicea was lukewarm.

The plague of a dull Christianity has invaded the Church. The curse grows worse when we fail to recognize the radical problem and seek to correct only a few of the more embarrassing symptoms—such as boring sermons, lifeless singing, stereotyped services. We need creative planning and structuring of our services, but we can adopt all the dramatic techniques from our latest seminars and imitate a lot of the clever innovations of successful churches and still be far from the solution to the real problem. The answer to a cold heart is a fresh vision of Jesus Christ, who alone can fill us with His Spirit and set our hearts on fire.

● *Slothful Stewardship*—The works of Sardis and Laodicea were not found perfect, this being due no doubt to their coldness of heart.

Spirit-filled Christians will take seriously the work of the
Lord. We should be preaching and teaching more these days
from such passages as the Parable of the Talents (Matt.
25:14-30). According to Jesus, not all the wickedness in town
is down at the brothel or bar; much of it is right in the hearts
of lazy, selfish church members. To the man who had been
squandering his talent Jesus said, "You wicked, lazy servant!"
Christ is angry with those churches and Christians who waste
their resources on themselves. This parable plainly teaches
that we are not ready to meet the Lord unless we are en-
thusiastically at work for Him. One way we will know revival
has come will be the transformation of the mediocre majority
of our members into joyous servants.

● *Seductive Heresy*—Pergamum and Thyatira yielded to
the teachings of the Balaamites and Nicolaitans. The first of
these were named for the false prophet who assisted Balaak
in corrupting the sons of Israel (Num. 22-25; 31:1-16). Their
first-century counterparts were advocates of moral compromise. So were the Nicolaitans, who brazenly taught that
salvation by grace allowed for freedom to sin. Pastors and
churches who stood by in silence while these heretics made a
travesty of Christian grace were being called to judgment in
this vision. Jude had this same "cheap grace" in mind when
he wrote of "godless men, who change the grace of our God
into a license for immorality and deny Jesus Christ our only
Sovereign and Lord" (v. 4).

Christians who fall into sin will usually repent or else they
will rewrite the Gospel to excuse their disobedience, and then
seek to convert others to their sensual ways. Unless a remnant of Spirit-empowered intercessors are recruited to wage

spiritual warfare, such apostles of darkness will reap a harvest of the young and naive in our churches.

● *Satanic Mysticism*—The Lord came down severely on Thyatira for tolerating a wicked movement, which He named for Jezebel, the notorious harlot-queen who peddled sorcery in Israel (I Kings 16-II Kings 9). The spirit of Jezebel can be identified by any number of characteristics: contemptuous of the holy; obsessed with sensuality and immorality; ambitious for control; charming and seductive; given over to witchcraft and strange powers.

A revival of mysticism is sweeping the world at this time. The learned and the unlearned are invading us with their sensational experiences. Dead and lifeless churches are most vulnerable. Psycho-spiritualists are coming from the universities, the backwoods and from foreign countries with their impressive visions and miracles to play their mindgames with nominal Christians. In their seminars, books and tapes they promise supernatural manifestations, prosperity according to one's mental powers of visualization, and peace in the paradise of this life. If the eyes of the angry Son of God blazed at Thyatira for allowing the strange fire of Jezebel to go unchallenged, how does He feel about all the strange mysticism invading the Church today?

May God give us some Elijahs who will devote themselves to prayer and fasting until they can take authority and confront such enemies of the Gospel and reveal them for what they are—servants of satan!

● *Smug Self-righteousness*—Laodicea boasted, "I am rich; I have acquired wealth and do not need a thing." But the Lord had a shocking reply: "You are wretched, pitiful, poor, blind and naked—and you don't even know it!" Their reek of self-satisfaction made the Lord sick. Smugness is so contagious that it can go through a staff and a church board and congregation like anthrax in a herd of cattle. The Lord excuses Himself from such a body and waits on the outside until they become sick of themselves. He will knock at the door, but He will not enter until they have accepted His prescription for their conceit: they must humble themselves and open the door to Him; they must renounce their false riches and receive His wealth; they must rend their worldly garments and trade them for a white robe to cover their shame; they must acknowledge their blindness so that He might apply the healing oil for them to see.

● *Lost Faith*—Five of the seven churches had not kept the faith. Yet they went right on functioning, growing more insensitive to the Holy Spirit and more vulnerable to the spirit of this age.

Someone has observed that if the Holy Spirit had withdrawn from the Apostolic church, at least ninety-five percent of all its operations would have ceased, and nearly everyone would have known the difference; but that if the Holy Spirit withdrew from the modern Church, at least ninety-five percent of our operations would go right on, and almost no one would know the difference.

## What Christ Commanded

● *Rouse from Your Sleep!*—To Sardis the Lord said, "Wake up!" The same call is going out to His sleeping body throughout North America. We must hear His voice and experience the kind of revival that will help us meet our destiny to shine in this dark, disintegrating world.

● *Repent of Your Sins!*—Five of the seven churches were commanded to repent. It is the merciful work of the Spirit to awaken the conscience and spirit and make it possible for one to repent. With the painful truth about ourselves there comes either a softening, humbling response of agreement or there will be a hardening, resisting spirit of resentment. Richard Owen Roberts insisted that in true repentance "one does not merely seek to escape the wrath of God or the guilt of conscience. The repentant person turns from *all* that displeases God toward that which pleases Him.[1]

The doctrine of repentance must return to pulpit and classroom. Without repentance there will be no genuine revival in our land.

● *Remember Your Past Glory!*—"Remember the height from which you have fallen!" Jesus told Ephesus. Some will need to look back for a perspective on the downward and wayward course they have traveled. When the Prodigal remembered how far he had fallen he came to his senses and repented. Proof of his repentance was his return to his father.

Many churches have a glorious history of revivals and evangelism and missions. But the spiritual tide changed along with the times. The Lord commands them to remember the former times of glory and power and freedom. Let the memory trigger a spirit of repentance that will lead to a restoration of the glory that was once real.

● *Receive your forsaken Lord!*—Jesus knocked on Laodicea's door. Today He calls to churches so obsessed with themselves that they have shut Him out completely. Do we realize that without Jesus at the center we cease to be His Church and that the spirit that drives us is not His Spirit at all?

Have we gradually crowded Him out? Will we now realize our need of Him and invite Him back in?

● *Revive your dying souls!*—Sardis was told, "Strengthen what you have before it dies" (*Phillips*). Sardis was caught up in its own glory and did not think it needed revival. Mercifully, the Lord gave one last call. "But if you do not wake up," He warned, "I will come as quietly as a thief to blow out your lamp and you'll go right on, never knowing what happened."

It's time to put everything else on hold and respond to the Spirit, Who is calling the churches to prepare for revival.

# The Conditions for Revival

Historians and prophets have been warning for decades that if civilization is to survive there must come another historic awakening. If a Sovereign God has promised to give revival in the last days, some ask, why is He not pouring out His Spirit and healing the land? Others point to growth among some churches and argue that we are having a revival.

But nearly all the evidence of another great revival in this country is still missing. Yet, as more and more believers are coming to realize God's promise of restoring His Church, I believe we are nearer than ever to meeting the conditions for revival.

## An Overwhelming Sense of Need

There is a growing awareness among leaders that we desperately need God's help. This is not to say that our sense of need is as widespread as it ought to be. We admit that some churchmen simply do not share a realization of the need for revival. Roberts again said:

> People have died of curable diseases without even knowing they needed a physician. Students have flunked out of college without ever having felt the need to study. Marriages have gotten all the way to the divorce courts before both partners realized there was a need. Men have lived seventy years on this earth and slipped into eternity without feeling any serious need to seek God.[2]

But there are encouraging signs that North American Christians are awakening to their greatest need. Richard Halverson, Chaplain of the United States Senate, observed, "There is a revival in our land of the *need* for revival."[3]

## A Growing Prayer Movement

A study of the great revivals in the Church reveals the common denominator to be that of prevailing prayer. In the powerful ministries of Wesley, Whitefield, Edwards and Finney, it is to be noted that preceding and accompanying these revivalists were bold but broken souls whom the Spirit of God had stirred to take hold of Him and not let go until He fulfilled His promise to do a new thing.

The most encouraging sign right now is the network of prayer warriors that God is forming. It appears that this increasing number of praying men and women consistently focus on the three major thrusts of the New Testament in their praying: (1) *Holiness*—they are repenting of their fleshly, carnal living and seeking the cleansing of the Holy Spirit; (2) *Fullness*—they are crying out for the empowerment of the Spirit, expecting to be restored to the authority and anointing known by the early Church; (3) *Evangelism*—they believe that the great heart of God yearns for the salvation of the masses, and they seek to enter His purpose for reaching them.

## A Passion for the Open Heavens

God warned His people in the past about conditions that would "close the heavens." He told them, "Be careful, or you will be enticed to turn away and worship other gods...Then the *Lord's* anger will burn against you, and he will *shut the heavens* so that it will not rain and the ground will yield no produce" (Deut. 11:16-17, emphasis added). God pleads with us today to meet the conditions that will allow Him to "hear from heaven" (II Chron. 7:14). Stephen Olford wrote:

> We notice that the opposite of revival is a closed heaven...Nothing can be more ominous than a closed heaven...On the other hand, when the Lord looks with favor on His people the windows of heaven are opened and blessing is poured forth in such measure that there is not enough room to receive it...[4]

Some time ago I was preaching in one of our Southwestern cities, and there was an unusual moving of the Holy Spirit in which most of the leaders of the church went forward to pray. At the close of the service a dear lady unburdened her heart.

> Not since I was a young woman have we experienced anything in this church like we have seen tonight. Most of our people don't even know about "the open heavens." But we've had a taste of revival, and tonight I promised God that I will pray as long as He gives me strength, and *I will not let Him go until the heavens open on our people!*

## A Healing of the Land

The moral and spiritual healing of America will have to begin with professing Christians. It will require the full flowing streams of the Spirit to wash away hurtful memories, heal infected spirits, fill up empty lives and make God's children a proper witness to His sanctifying grace.

But revival will not stop with the Church. When the diseased, disobedient Church is healed, the mighty work of revival will extend to the lost. When church members are delivered from resentments and grudges, drug addicts will also find deliverance. When Christians are cleansed from lust, homosexuals will find healing. Many diseased victims go on in their suffering because God's people are caught up in the pleasures and cares of life, oblivious to the power of God to be released through the Church to a needy world.

All great revivals have penetrated the moral and social fabric of the nation. People stop the sin business and turn to righteousness. The converted pay their bills and make restitution. Values and lifestyles change. The crime rate drops. The marvelous works of God make the headlines as the whole land develops a new God-consciousness.

A strong faith is growing in the hearts of God's praying remnant. They are praying that the Church will catch a new vision of the glory of Jesus Christ and that the Spirit will give it an ear to hear what He has to say. Only then will the Church repent of its self-righteousness and face its spiritual bankruptcy. Her Lord will then heal her blindness, clothe her nakedness and arm her with the glory of His Spirit. The world will then ask, "Who is this that appears like the dawn, fair as the moon, bright as the sun, majestic as the stars in procession?" (Song of Sol. 6:10).

# Notes

1. Richard Owen Roberts, *Revival!* (Tyndale House, 1982), p. 75.

2. *Ibid.*, p. 63.

3. Reported by Armin R. Gesswein in *The Alliance Witness*, Vol. 121, No. 1.

4. Stephen Olford, *Lord, Open the Heavens! (Harold Shaw Publishers, 1980), pp. 34-35.*

# Chapter 4

# Rekindling the Flames

*I have been reminded of your sincere faith, which first
lived in your grandmother Lois and in your mother
Eunice and, I am persuaded, now lives in you also. For
this reason I remind you to fan into flame the gift of
God, which is in you through the laying on of my hands.
For God did not give us a spirit of timidity, but a spirit
of power, of love and of self-discipline.*

*So do not be ashamed to testify about our Lord, or
ashamed of me his prisoner. But join with me in suffering for the gospel, by the power of God, who has saved
us and called us to a holy life...*

II Timothy 1:5-9

Suffering alone in Rome's Mamertine prison, the apostle
Paul had more to think about than his own personal needs
and approaching execution. Although Luke was with him, he
longed to see the face of his spiritual son Timothy, who was
in charge of the church at Ephesus.

When Paul had visited the town of Lystra on his first missionary journey he had discovered there an unusual young man. Building on Timothy's rich spiritual heritage, Paul was likely the one who had led the boy to a personal knowledge of Christ. The apostle had lavished his prayers upon the lad and discipled him in all aspects of the Christian faith. During his second visit, Paul had recognized in Timothy maturity of character, outstanding spiritual gifts and a growing vision of the Kingdom of God. As the older man laid hands on the younger man in holy consecration, Timothy had been filled with the Holy Spirit.

For a number of years Timothy had traveled with Paul and demonstrated the power of the Holy Spirit both in personal living and in public ministry. On a number of occasions he had served as Paul's envoy to the churches. In Berea and Thessalonica he had been left to follow up the work of the apostle and to solidify and strengthen the believers. Paul's confidence in Timothy is seen in having sent him to Corinth to help the church through much tension. We are not surprised then to see him as the shepherd of the church in Ephesus.

But something had happened to Timothy through the years. It is clear from Paul's letter that the fire was burning low in the younger man's heart.

## Quenching the Spirit

John the Baptist declared that Jesus would baptize His followers "with the Holy Spirit and with fire" (Matt. 3:11). Jesus came as a redeeming revolutionary to set the world on fire

(Luke 12:49). Pentecostal flames exploded in the hearts of early Christians, and they were set aglow to do the mighty work Christ had commissioned them to do (Acts 1:1-4).

True Christianity is a holy fire set in the heart of the believer. But as General William Booth, founder of the Salvation Army, once wrote his officers, "The tendency of fire is to go out, so watch the fire on the altar of your hearts." John Wesley confessed, "When I fail to fast and pray, I soon lose my spiritual heat and passion." Richard Newton acknowledged, "The principal cause of my leanness and unfruitfulness is owing to an unaccountable backwardness to pray." We all find it easier to guard the ashes of our past religious experiences than to tend the flames of spiritual power. The fire can go out. If it happened to Timothy, it can happen to you and to me. As Paul directed Timothy, so we too are called to shake off the ashes of our traditions and acknowledge coldness of heart. In brokenness and humility we must ask the Lord to pull together the coals remaining and fan them into flame. It is His desire to make "his servants flames of fire" (Heb. 1:7).

"Do not quench the Spirit," Paul warned (I Thes. 5:19, RSV). "Do not put out the Spirit's fire," says the NIV. The word "quench" means "to subdue, to sit on, to stifle, to choke, to suppress, to dampen, to repress." Christians always face the danger of putting out the fire of the Holy Spirit. This does not mean that the Spirit of God necessarily leaves us; it means that He is restricted within us and is not free to work the purpose of God in our hearts. We can stifle the life of the Spirit in us in a number of ways: by ignoring His passion in us for communion with God; by substituting personal interests for His hunger in us for the Word of God; by sitting on (putting off) His direction to us to minister to someone in need; by giving in to doubt instead of accepting the faith the Spirit would give us for some cause that would advance the Kingdom of God; by forgetting that the Christian life is lived successfully only as we learn to relate properly to the indwelling Holy Spirit. His work in us is not automatic—either it is repressed or renewed according to our personal response to Him.

The fire of the Spirit can be put out by sins of omission as well as by sins of active disobedience. In Timothy's case, look carefully at verses seven and eight and note what happens when the fire goes out. There is always a subtle acclimation to the environment of the world. Timothy had succumbed to fear. He had acquired a "spirit of timidity." Lloyd Ogilvie noted that the word for "timidity" (*deilia*) is a term always used in a bad sense. And he pointed out that the word "spirit" used with it means a pervading mood, attitude, mode of thinking.

In other words, the spirit of fear cripples us with caution and reserve. It limits what we are willing to attempt to only those things we are sure we can do in our own strength....The spirit of fear manifests itself in a panic over criticism and unhealthy concern over what others think. Fearing failure, we attempt very little. The spirit of fear can also spread to groups and even pervade a church congregation. When leaders are more concerned about being adequate than being on fire with Christ, their timidity and cowardice water down the robust preaching of the Gospel. As a result, the dynamic impact of the church on society is lost.[1]

Timothy's spirit of fear was absolutely foreign to that of the freedom and joy and power known by the apostles who were filled and led by the Holy Spirit. Such a dark mood of negativism and unbelief that seizes one's spirit and clouds any sense of direction and smothers inspiration and produces worry and embarrassment and defeat *is not of* God! But God does have the answer.

# Rekindling the Flames

Timothy was in spiritual trouble, and the old apostle knew it. Paul wrote and gave it to him straight. He prescribed for his son in the faith the only solution for a cold, fearful, defeated heart. No, he did not tell Timothy to get with it and double his efforts. He did not direct him back to the university for another academic degree. He did not recommend a change of pastorates. He did not even suggest that after all the years of stressful labors in the ministry, Timothy needed a sabbatical to travel to another continent. While all these measures have merit at appropriate times, not one of them can rekindle the fire of the Holy Spirit in the believer's soul.

No, Timothy had to do one thing: *return to the source of Christian power!* Timothy needed to be renewed in the divine fullness he received when Paul first laid hands on him in prayer for the power of the Holy Spirit.

Charles G. Finney was mightily used by God in the nineteenth century to help shape American Christianity's views on the work of the Holy Spirit in the life of the believer. His teachings on "the filling of the Holy Spirit" and "the baptism of the Holy Spirit" have contributed to the various views—the Wesleyan-Holiness, the Pentecostal-Charismatic, the Keswick and the common evangelical view—for most of the twentieth century. Although Finney would not fit perfectly into any one of the four molds, all are in debt to the evangelist. James Gilchrist Lawson wrote of God' great accomplishments through this one who knew the source of his power:

> During the year 1857-58 over a hundred thousand persons were led to Christ as the direct or indirect result of Finney's labors, while five hundred thousand persons professed conversion in the great revival which began in his meetings...It was found by actual research that over eighty-five in every hundred persons professing conversion to Christ in Finney's meetings remained true to God.[2]

The personal testimony of one so mightily used of God to revive the Church and reach the lost should be considered. In his autobiography Finney described "the mighty baptism of the Holy Spirit," which gave him power to become what God called him to be:

> The Holy Spirit descended upon me in a manner that seemed to go through me body and soul. I could feel the impression like a wave of electricity, going through and through me. Indeed it seemed to come in waves of liquid love...It seemed like the very breath of God....No words can express the wonderful love that was shed abroad in my heart. I wept aloud with joy and love; and I do not know but I should say I literally bellowed out the unutterable gushings of my heart.[3]

Finney also testified to the effects of this experience:

> I immediately found myself endued with such power from on high that a few words dropped here and there to individuals were the means of their immediate conversion. My words seemed to fasten like barbed arrows in the souls of men. They cut like a sword, they broke the heart like a hammer.[4]

But Finney also learned how easily the fire can go out:

> Sometimes I would find myself in a great measure empty of this power. I would go out and visit and find that I made no saving impression...After humbling myself and crying out for help, the power would return upon me with all its freshness.[5]

The powerful evangelist from New York took the teachings of Jesus seriously concerning the Holy Spirit (Luke 11:9-13). He insisted that it is not hard for a Christian to be filled with the Spirit, provided that he wants to be filled with the Spirit more than he wants anything else.

# Prevailing in Prayer

The experiences of prayer and the renewings of the Holy Spirit are so interrelated that sometimes we are confused about the cause and the effect. The truth is that only praying hearts are filled with the Holy Spirit. And it is equally true that only Spirit-filled hearts can prevail in prayer.

It is the baptizing fullness of the Spirit that sets our hearts on fire to pray. Churches are not revived through preaching alone; it takes prayer, Spirit-anointed prayer. Only those Christians who are full of God's Spirit are able to engage in such praying; only Christians who are praying can retain such fullness.

Education and personality and sincerity can go a long ways in promoting revival and evangelism and growth in the Church, but these cannot set hearts on fire or convict the lost of their need of Christ. This is the work of the Holy Spirit, but He does not do it except as we pray.

Our Lord left His followers a marvelous legacy of prayer. He spent more time instructing on the principles, the practice and the power of prayer than on any other subject. Most of His teachings and promises concerning the Holy Spirit took place within the context of His emphasis on prayer.

If Jesus held the attention of His men at any point, they were absolutely amazed when He spoke on prayer. This was due not only to what He had to say but also because of the mighty works of power in His life, which He attributed to prayer. Whatever He asked, He believed He would receive. And, sooner or later, it was His.

Jesus would often leave the crowd and His own disciples to go alone and pray to the Father in secret. Before long, however, His secret praying was rewarded openly: the blind received their sight, the lame walked, the lepers were healed, the deaf heard, the dead were raised, the demon-possessed were liberated, the glorious Gospel of the Kingdom was preached in great power and many believed in the Savior and received eternal life—all because of the mysterious anointing of the Holy Spirit upon Jesus for a life of prayer.

The Lord taught His disciples that prayer would work for them just as it worked for Him. He taught that it is prayer that cuts the channels for the flowing of the Spirit of Pentecost. He showed that prayer sets the stage for the mighty workings of God in His Church.

The first Pentecostal effusion was an eloquent announcement that Jesus, who had been crucified and raised from the dead, was now exalted to the place of sovereign power at the Father's right hand. Moreover, the outpouring of the Holy Spirit declared that the Sovereign Christ had now returned and released Himself into His Church in the Person of the Omnipresent Spirit to indwell His people and convict the world. With the outpouring of the Spirit, Christ set His messengers on fire and began His world revolution.

The Pentecostal gale that blew into the Upper Room brought forth a new people—a people alive, transformed, filled, empowered to be Christ's witnesses in a world that waited for the mercies of God. The Holy Spirit truly is the Spirit of resurrection. He is the only One who can bring life out of death. He is the only force that can raise sinners from the grave and impart to them the eternal life of Christ. The Holy Spirit alone can raise churches from the dead.

It all begins in the Upper Room. It does not require large numbers to form the critical mass for a congregational revival. Like Gideon's band, the Upper Room approach will always thin out the ranks. But the few who are left must covenant with the Lord and one another *to pray until revival comes.* Prayer warriors today must become as shameless in their persistence for a divine visitation as the importuning widow with the unjust judge (Luke 18:1-8). Sooner or later, the winds of the Spirit will start to blow. Cold hearts will begin to thaw. Scales will fall from blinded eyes. More and more Christians will be given an ear to hear what the Spirit is saying to the Church. As obedience becomes the order of the day, the fires of revival will fall and once more the hearts of God's people will be set ablaze.

## Notes

1. Lloyd Ogilvie, *Twelve Steps to Living without Fear* (Word, 1987), p. 102.

2. James Gilchrist Lawson, *Deeper Experiences of Famous Christians* (Warner Press, Anderson, Indiana, 1911), p. 175.

3. Charles G. Finney, *Charles G. Finney: An Autobiography* (Fleming H. Revell, 1980), pp. 20-21.

4. Charles G. Finney, *Power from on High: A Selection of Articles on the Spirit-filled Life* (Christian Literature Crusade, n.d.), p. 10.

5. *Ibid.*

# Chapter 5

# The Invisible War

*Finally, be strong in the Lord and in his mighty power. Put on the full armor of God so that you can take your stand against the devil's schemes. For our struggle is not against flesh and blood, but against the rulers, against the authorities, against the powers of this dark world and against the spiritual forces of evil in the heavenly realms. Therefore put on the full armor of God, so that when the day of evil comes, you may be able to stand your ground...*

Ephesians 6:10-13

The spiritual conflict of the ages grows more violent as civilization moves closer to the end. Behind the signs of the times there rages an invisible war. The sweeping changes politically, socially, morally, physically, economically and spiritually are but symptoms of what Alexander Solzhenitsyn called "a fight of cosmic proportions." He stated his belief that the forces of evil have already begun their final offensive.

In spiritual warfare, just as in physical conflict, there is the ebb and flow of battle. Territories are won and lost. Strongholds are established and destroyed. Nations rise and fall. There are wars and rumors of wars. Terror increases around the globe. With droughts, famines, inflation and an increasing population, the struggle for survival grows more desperate each year over a great part of our planet. Add to these things a wholesale disregard for the Word of God against murder, stealing, lying, adultery, homosexuality, divorce and idolatry— these prohibitions are given for the good of the human race— and we can see the horrible consequences in crowded prisons, broken homes, drug addiction, the curse of AIDS and the collapse of economies trying to pay for the sins of a society that refuses to repent. Little wonder that Jesus forefold the panic of the last days because of such dreadful conditions (Luke 21:26).

Many intelligent observers of the times believe that civilization is staggering toward a dangerous climax. Dostoevsky predicted the death of Western civilization, and gave as the sole reason that it had lost Jesus Christ. Francis Schaeffer warned of the collapse of the West for the same reason. Charles Colson has claimed that we are now entering "the new dark ages."

> "Dark Age" is a strong term, I recognize that. Yet in recent years I've had a growing sense of storm clouds on the horizon. Material obsession paralyzes the West and political repression grips the East. Scandals and scams are commonplace in our world. Men and women trade character for cash and sacrifice commitment on the altar of selfishness. Politicians, preachers and professionals prey on the weak. Wars and rumors of wars fill our airwaves. Terrorists and

hostages are nightly news. Nuclear weapons, plastic ex-
plosives, handguns and chemical warfare fuel our fears. All
around us crime rises, moral values decline and families frag-
ment.[1]

# Called to War

The world is at war, and God has called the Church to
engage in decisive conflict. Nearly half of the earth's masses
have not heard the Gospel of Jesus Christ because "the god
of this age has blinded the minds of unbelievers" (II Cor. 4:4)
and because the Church, like Jonah running from the call of
God to proclaim His Word to a wicked city, is fast asleep
while the storm of final destruction is gathering.

Before the church can complete her task of taking the
Gospel to the whole world she must experience a full-scale
awakening. Such a revival will require men and women from
all walks of life to give themselves to prayer and fasting and
the learning of spiritual warfare.

## Our Strong Adversary

It is tempting for Christians to focus on symptoms and or-
ganizations as they prepare for spiritual conflict, but Paul cautioned that "our struggle is not against flesh and blood, but
against the rulers, against the authorities, against the powers
of this dark world and against the spiritual forces of evil in the
heavenly realms" (Eph. 6;12). Paul would enlighten the
Church to a kingdom of fallen spirits that is ruled over by
satan, and it has a dangerous chain of command.

When the apostle said concerning satan that "we are not ignorant of his devices" (II Cor. 2:11, *KJV*), he was not speaking for most Christians. So many in the Church are unaware of the way the Enemy works. He resorts to unfair tactics, and will in any way possible seduce, corrupt, torment, accuse, harass, intimidate and destroy anyone he can, especially a child of God.

Satan is not omnipotent (only God is!), but he has supernatural abilities so that, apart from the power of Christ, none of us can match his strength.

Satan is not omniscient (only God is!), but he is superintelligent and very subtle in his study of the Church and the saints. But he does have to study us and learn our weaknesses, while God knows all about us instantly and perfectly.

Satan is not omnipresent (only God is!), but he operates a world-wide network of evil that is highly organized and well supplied.

We are called to go to war against such an Enemy. Not only are we commanded to stand against him defensively; we are ordered to invade his territory, unmask and reveal him, bind him, and release his captives.

## Our Sovereign Lord

And how are we to do all of this? *In the mighty Name of Jesus! In the incomparable power of the Holy Spirit! By ruling with Christ in prayer! "All authority in heaven and on earth has been given to me," declared Jesus (Matt. 28:18). In power He commands us to go and invade the kingdom of darkness, to bind Satan, to liberate lives, to declare the glorious Gospel—all in His strong name. For this purpose He has made us kings and priests (I Pet. 2:5,*

*9; Rev. 1:6). In this present age Christ is not yet ruling with a scepter; He rules by prayer. It is in intercessory prayer that the Church discovers the mighty power committed to her by our Sovereign Lord. At Calvary, Jesus disarmed the principalities and powers; in the Upper Room we enforce that victory. We are, here and now, destined to rule with Christ against all that stands in the way of His Kingdom. Intercessory prayer warriors must grow bold and decree the destruction of hypocrisy and apathy in the Church. With the praise of God on our lips and the Sword of the Lord in our hands we are called to inflict vengeance on the rulers of darkness by tearing down their strongholds and rescuing their victims.*

May God give such a band of bold prayer warriors in every church in America who will follow their Sovereign Commander to victory. Francis Frangipane wrote:

Of all the names our Heavenly Father could have given His Son, it is most significant that He chose the name "Jesus," for Jesus is the Greek form of "Joshua," who was the Hebrew general who led the people into warfare. To be prepared for greater victories, we need a greater revelation of Jesus Christ; we need to see Him as He will be revealed in the last moments of this age: a Holy Warrior, dressed for battle.[2]

# Dressed for Battle

A true spiritual warrior is different from the rank-and-file soldier. A true warrior *thinks* like a warrior, *dresses* like a warrior, *obeys* like a warrior and *fights* like a warrior. A true warrior goes to battle with a will to win.

## The Armor of God

The spiritual warrior's armor is "of God," said Paul, meaning that the equipment is designed for us and fitted on us personally by the Lord. Actually, Christ Himself is our armor, and Paul had a dramatic way of illustrating spiritual warfare in the power of Christ.

● *The Girdle of Truth*—The Roman soldier wore a wide leather belt around his waist. It was basic, and formed the foundation for much of the remaining armor. Jesus Christ is everything to the believer. Paul said that He has "become for us wisdom from God—that is, our righteousness, holiness and redemption" (I Cor. 1:30).

Jesus is the very personification of truth. His favorite title for the Holy Spirit was "the Spirit of truth." Those who would follow Christ to victory must be made free from all treachery and falsehood. Prayer warriors are children of the light whose natures undergo a thorough cleansing by the spirit of truth. Satan will hold us hostage wherever lying and deception occur. We must tell the truth on our income tax forms, job applications, insurance claims and on all occasions and circumstances.

● *The Breastplate of Righteousness*—We are taught in the book of Romans that God made Christ our righteousness (our justification) in order that the Spirit might work in us the likeness of Jesus (our sanctification). This is a mighty armor against satan as we walk in such assurance of salvation by faith. And how much greater our assurance when the Holy

Spirit is allowed to purify our hearts! Great harm is caused the Evil One and his dark kingdom when the prayer warrior comes before the Throne of Grace with the confidence of forgiveness and cleansing in Christ.

● *The Gospel Boots*—We are to be "strong in the Lord and in his might power." We are to stand in Christ, not in ourselves. In hand-to-hand combat, the soldier must be shod with boots having cleats to give him sure footing. One slip and he could be dead. Those who prevail in spiritual warfare must stand on the solid ground of the powerful Gospel of Jesus Christ.

● *The Shield of Faith*—The skilled prayer warrior learns to keep his eyes on Jesus, "the author and perfecter of our faith" (Heb. 12:2). When satan hurls his darts of doubt and discouragement, we must raise the shield of faith and "extinguish all the flaming arrows of the evil one." When satan comes at us preaching circumstances and citing past failures, it is time to quote the Word and stop the onslaughts. "This is the victory that has overcome the world, even our faith" (I John 5:4).

● *The Helmet of Salvation*—Satan dreads our helmet because it is the symbol of hope (I Thes. 5:8). Our helmet of protection is the glorious mystery, "which is Christ in [us], the hope of glory" (Col 1:17). We demonstrate strong hope in battle, knowing we are not dependent on ourselves. Paul wrote, "May the God of hope fill you with all joy and peace as you trust in him, so that you may overflow with hope by the power of the Holy Spirit" (Rom. 15:13).

● *The Sword of the Spirit*—Christ is the Eternal Word (John 1:1). If God has spoken to us through Christ, then

Christ is God speaking to us. His Word is the powerful work of the Holy Spirit saving, cleansing, reviving and empowering us for battle. The Spirit does not work in and through us apart from the Word. Jesus is our example in waging warfare against satan in the power of the indispensable Word of God (Matt. 4:1-11).

● *Praying in the Holy Spirit*—In verse eighteen, Paul urged a final piece of armor: "And pray in the Spirit on all occasions with all kinds of prayers and request." Some controversy accompanies the subject of praying in the Spirit, but for this writer it means three things: (1) The Holy Spirit enlightens my understanding so that I can pray according to the will of God; (2) The Holy Spirit energizes my spirit so that I can pray and not faint; and (3) The Holy Spirit emboldens my faith so that I can ask largely and not be denied. Satan dreads the prayers of the Spirit-anointed intercessors more than all the other religious exercises of the Church.

# Triumphant in Conflict

Those who pray in the power of the Holy Spirit are not shadow-boxing; they are putting to flight the demonic forces that hinder Christ's work. Our Lord promised that "the gates of hell shall not prevail" against His Church (Matt. 16:18, KJV).

More and more slumbering Christians are hearing the Spirit say, "Wake up, O sleeper, rise from the dead, and Christ will shine on you" (Eph. 5:14). Christ is blowing reveille for a mighty invasion of the Enemy's territory at this hour. And how the forces of hell fear ths awakening! It assures the frustration of satanic strategies, the destruction of demonic strongholds and the retreat of the kingdom of darkness.

The long spiritual drought in this country must soon end with a supernatural opening of the heavens. Our Captain of the Hosts is sounding His war cry against evil. He is training His armies on earth to move in harmony with the Heavenly Hosts. "The Lord will march out like a mighty man, like a warrior he will stir up his zeal; with a shout he will raise the battle cry and will triumph over his enemies" (Isa. 42:13). Satan fears the Invincible Captain and His mighty armies more than anything else. This is why the spiritual forces of evil are trembling at this hour. They know that the Sovereign One is about to lead His forces in an unparalleled sweep against darkness. "Then will the eyes of the blind be opened and the ears of the deaf unstopped. Then will the lame leap like a deer, and the mute tongue shout for joy. Water will gush forth in the wilderness and streams in the desert. The burning sand will become a pool, the thirsty ground bubbling springs. In the haunts where jackals once lay, grass and reeds and papyrus will grow. And a highway will be there; it will be called the Way of Holiness. The unclean will not journey on it...only the redeemed will walk there, and the ransomed of the Lord will return. They will enter Zion with singing; everlasting joy will crown their heads. Gladness and joy overtake them, and sorrow and sighing will flee away" (Isa. 35:5-10).

Only this kind of revival will quench the thirst of the people of God and prepare them for the greatest harvest of souls in the history of the Church. Such a marvelous work of God will, I believe, prepare His people for the return of our Lord Jesus Christ.

May God bless each and every church body across this continent with prayer warriors armed with invincible weapons—the blood of the Lamb, the testimony of the Word and the fullness of the Holy Spirit—who will engage the enemy at this urgent hour to prove the victory and glory of our Sovereign Christ.

# Notes

1. Charles Colson, *Against the Night* (Servant Publications, 1989), p. 9.

2. Francis Frangipane, *The Three Battlegrounds* (River of Life Ministries, 1989), p. 45.

# Chapter 6

# "Clothed With Power"

*Jesus returned in the power of the Spirit....And they were astonished at his doctrine: for his word was with power...*

Luke 4:14, 32, *KJV*

*I am going to send you what my Father has promised; but stay in the city until you have been clothed with power from on high.*

Luke 24:49

*But you will receive power when the Holy Spirit comes on you; and you will be my witnesses...*

Acts 1:8

*For the kingdom of God is not a matter of talk but of power.*

I Corinthians 4:20

It is the conviction of this writer that more and more Christians will start to take seriously the power of the Holy Spirit

over the next few years. Many who have been going through
the motions of Christianity are going to grow hungry for its
power.

All spiritual failure, despite the moral, doctrinal or emotional symptoms, can be traced to one thing: failure to relate
properly to the Holy Spirit as Jesus taught.

Those who receive eternal life are also called to enjoy
abundant life. "If we live by the Spirit," said Paul, "let us also
walk by the Spirit" (Gal. 5:25, *RSV*). Since we are made alive
in Christ, we are to consciously and actively and prayerfully
press forth each day into the dynamics of the Spirit-led life.

The clearest outline for the believer's walk in the Spirit is
the life of our Lord. Throughout His entire ministry He is
shown to live as man completely under the control of the
Spirit of God. He spent much of His time preparing His disciples for the role of the Spirit in their lives. Only as they were
filled and controlled by the Holy Spirit could He continue His
life through them after His resurrection and ascension, as He
had promised. So He ordered them to stay in the city after
His ascension until they were filled with the Holy Spirit. The
Spirit would come to be *with* them, and He would dwell *in*
them. He would guide them into all truth. He would remind
them of all that Jesus had said. The Spirit would enlighten,
energize and inspire them for prayer so that they would come
directly to the Father on the authority of Christ and know
what to ask for. The Father would freely give whatever they
asked for in Christ's name. The secret of knowing what to ask
for, as well as the faith for asking, would be found in their
relationship with the Holy Spirit. *"He will bring glory to me
by taking from what is mine and making it known to you,"*
promised Jesus (John 16:14).

By the time Jesus ascended to the Father the disciples were absolutely convinced that their first duty was to wait in Jerusalem until they were "clothed with power from on high." The verb "clothed" as used in Luke 24:49 and in other ways conveys at least three different meanings: (1) To be dressed in such a manner that one's nakedness is covered, so that there is no longer shame or embarrassment, and so that one is now properly attired and presentable; (2) To be "dressed up" or arrayed in such fine garments as to identify with and give credit to a generous provider, such as a loving father who takes pride in his well-dressed children; (3) To be robed up in authority, like a magistrate who dons the black gown before taking his seat of power to rule.

We need to see in these three shades of meaning some special relationships the believer has with Christ through the power of the Holy Spirit.

# The Robe of Righteousness

Before our sins can be graciously covered, they must be painfully uncovered. It is the work of the Holy Spirit, said Jesus, "to convict the world of guilt in regard to sin and righteousness and judgment" (John 16:8). When the Spirit of God convicts us of sin He strikes our hearts with the Word of God in such an awakening that we see at last our shameful, undone condition. Only then can we discard our false covering of self-righteous works and avail ourselves of the only true covering for our sins—the righteousness of Christ. When Adam and Eve disobeyed God, they experienced guilt. At first they "sewed fig leaves together and made coverings for themselves" (Gen. 3:7). When God sought them out and dealt with them, they were convicted of their sin and stood before Him shamefully exposed. But when the guilty pair repented, "the Lord God made garments of skin for Adam and his wife and clothed them" (Gen. 3:21).

Our gracious heavenly Father paid an extravagant price to clothe us in the righteousness of His Son. Claiming that nothing reveals the gravity of our sin like the cross, John R. W. Stott wrote:

> It is impossible for us to face Christ's cross with integrity and not to feel ashamed of ourselves. Apathy, selfishness and complacency blossom everywhere else in the world except at the cross. There these noxious weeds shrivel and die. They are seen for the tatty, poisonous things they are. For if there was no way by which the righteous God could righteously forgive our unrighteousness, except that He should bear it Himself in Christ, it must be serious indeed. It is only when we see this that, stripped of our self-righteousness and self-satisfaction, we are ready to put our trust in Jesus Christ as the Savior we urgently need.[1]

The genius of the Gospel is seen in its power not only to cover the believing sinner with the righteousness of Christ but also to transform the heart of the one covered. Paul wrote, "God made him who had no sin to be sin for us, so that in him we might become the righteousness of God" (II Cor. 5:21). But we need to understand that our salvation through Christ begins with a covering for the sinner and not a compromise with sin. Those who are covered are transformed. The justified are regenerated. Otherwise, as Dietrich Bonhoeffer warned, we come forth with a "cheap grace."

> Cheap grace means the justification of sin without the justification of the sinner. Cheap grace is the preaching of forgiveness without requiring repentance, baptism without

church discipline, Communion without confession....Cheap grace is grace without discipleship, grace without the cross.[2]

In Jesus's story about the prodigal son, He pictured a compassionate father running to meet the returning boy "while he was still a long way off" (Luke 15:20). After the father had welcomed his son with hugs and kisses, he ordered his servants, "Quick! Bring the best robe and put it on him. Put a ring on his finger and sandals on his feet. Bring the fattened calf and kill it. Let's have a feast and celebrate. *For this son of mine was dead and is alive again; he was lost and is found*" *(vv. 22-24, emphasis added). The father called for a celebration because of his joy over the change that had taken place in his son.*

The proof that we are clothed in the righteousness of Christ will be the forthcoming works of righteousness—a beginning of the Spirit's reproduction of Christ's life in us. This is the first step to true Christian power.

## The Garments of Praise

"Awake, awake, put on your strength, O Zion; put on your beautiful garments" (Isa. 52:1, *RSV*). When we are clothed in the righteousness of Christ we are dressed up for a true celebration of praise to the God of our salvation. In filling us with His Spirit the Lord gives us "a crown of beauty instead of ashes, the oil of gladness instead of mourning, and a garment of praise instead of a spirit of despair" (Isa. 61:3).

Luke reported that "Jesus, full of joy through the Holy Spirit," praised the Father intensely (Luke 10:21). The Holy

Spirit powerfully used the praises of early Christians to attract and convict the multitudes on the day of Pentecost (Acts 2:4-12). Marvelous things happen in gatherings of worship where believers are awestruck in the glory of God's Presence. Carnal souls are stabbed awake to a sense of undoneness, and they cry for cleansing. Sinners repent of their sins and turn to Christ. Those in bondage are brought to a glorious freedom. Young people hear and respond to God's call to Christian service. The scales fall from blinded eyes and spiritual ears are opened to hear what the Spirit is saying to the Church.

But in those churches where there is little or no sense of the glory of God the opposite is true. Nothing happens except by human ability. The tragic spiritual depression is not even realized because the religious are preoccupied with their own thoughts and ways and plans.

Revival begins when the Spirit of light uncovers the desolate condition and when Christians respond in repentance. When the Spirit applies the Word and the blood of Christ, new life will burst forth. At some point revival will express itself in glorious praise. Lloyd Ogilvie wrote:

> God does not need our praise as much as we need to give it. Praise is like a thermostat that opens the heart to flow in communion with God. Hallowing God's name is enumerating His attributes. When we think magnificently about God's nature we become open to experience afresh His glory in our lives...The more we praise the Lord, the more we will be able to think His thoughts after Him...He loosens the tissues of our brains to become channels of His Spirit.

> Praise is the ultimate level of relinquishment. When we praise God for not only all He is but what He is doing in our lives, we reach a liberating state of surrender.[3]

Our Creator designed our human spirits primarily for worship and praise. Let us then come to Christ to be cleansed, filled and clothed in power that we might "continually offer to God a sacrifice of praise" (Heb. 13:15). "I will bless the *Lord* at all times," the psalmist said, "his praise shall continually be in my mouth" (Ps. 34:1, *RSV*). "Rejoice in the Lord always," urged Paul, "I will say it again; Rejoice" (Philip. 4:4). We should greet each new day with praise to God, who gives life. Our first moments of consciousness should find us pouring forth expressions of thanksgiving. Such a holy exercise so early will preclude the subtle negative thoughts that lead to doubts, complaints, irritations and depression.

May the Lord grant us the kind of revival that will deliver our drowsy spirits out of their stupor and cause us to bathe in the "river whose streams make glad the city of God" (Ps. 46:4). Oh, to see the Church all dressed up once more in her garments of praise!

# The Mantle of Power

Jesus made it crystal clear that His disciples were not prepared to do His work until they were "clothed with power" by His Spirit. When they had been filled with His Spirit, they would "do even greater things than" He had done (John 14:12-13).

In studying the promise of the departing Christ to His disciples, it is very helpful to consider the parallel story of Elijah preparing Elisha to inherit his authority to carry on his work (II Kings 2:1-15).

## The Devoted Disciple

Elijah visited Elisha while the younger man was plowing in the fields (I Kings 19:19-21). When the old prophet called Elisha, the young man first replied, "Let me kiss my father and my mother, and then I will follow you." Since this implied more than a good-bye ceremony, Elijah told him in effect to forget it. Elisha returned home, but he could never find rest until he sold out completely and joined Elijah in a full-time commitment.

As Elijah's time came to depart this life, he put Elisha through a final test. Three times—at Gilgal, at Bethel and at Jericho—the master suggested a convenient point at which the younger man might stop short of going all the way to the fullness of power by which to carry on the work of ministry as Elijah's true successor. "Tarry here," Elijah would suggest. At any of the three places Elisha could have joined a class of student prophets who were preparing for the service of Jehovah. He would dwell with them in respect and influence.

"As the Lord lives, and as you yourself live, I will not leave you," was Elisha's firm response. Nothing in the world had moved the younger man like the power of God at work in Elijah. He had seen the fire of God ablaze in the old prophet and he would never be satisfied until that same fire had fallen on him. The glory of God on the master was Elisha's magnificent obsession. Whatever else he might miss in life, Elisha knew that he could not afford to miss the splendor of God in his own ministry. He would keep in step with his master to the very end.

Jesus invites, "If anyone is thirsty, let him come to me and drink. Whoever believes in me, as the Scripture has said, streams of living water will flow from within him." And then John added, "By this he meant the Spirit, whom those who believed in him were later to receive" (John 7:37-39). The crucial condition for being filled with the Spirit is an all-consuming thirst for Christ, a longing for His Presence, an ache for His righteousness, a passion for His power by which to do His work.

Those who do not so thirst after Christ can find convenient levels at which to depart from following hard after Him. In so doing, they will have to settle for something other than the fullness of the Holy Spirit. Some will even turn to some other spirit than the Spirit of Christ.

## The Critical Question

When Elijah realized that Elisha really meant business, he said to him, "Tell me, what can I do for you before I am taken from you?" (II Kings 2:9). In his response Elisha decided to test the validity of the inheritance law relating to the firstborn (Deut. 21:17)—a double portion of the father's estate was assigned the firstborn by which to carry on the family name and business. "Let me inherit a double portion of your spirit," Elisha asked. The old prophet was pleased, and he said, "You have asked a difficult thing," meaning that Elisha had made a critical request, that he had put his heart on the very purpose of God, and that what he was seeking was within the power of God alone to grant. There was one condition, however, by which Elisha could receive a double portion of the Spirit of God: *he must keep his eyes on his master to the very end.*

We do not accidentally stagger into the fullness and power of the Holy Spirit. God is not capricious when it comes to measuring out the power of His Spirit. He will stir us to an awareness of our need, but unless we want divine fullness with all our souls we'll wander off to other things in emptiness and defeat. The more thirsty we grow for the Spirit of God in our lives the more we will ask and seek and knock for His fullness (Luke 11:9-13). The Father wants so very much to give us more and more of His Spirit, but not until we surrender everything will we know the baptizing fullness of the Holy Spirit and fire that Jesus promised.

## The Mantle of Power

Elisha kept his eyes on his master and was at last allowed to witness the phenomenon. "As they were walking along and talking together, suddenly a chariot of fire and horses of fire appeared and separated the two of them, and Elijah went up to heaven in a whirlwind. Elijah saw this and cried out, 'My father! My father!' "

When Elisha's emotions had somewhat subsided, he looked down at his feet and saw that Elijah had left his old mantle for him. In an explosion of joy, he tore off his own cloak and draped himself with Elijah's mantle.

Throughout the Old Testament we notice that one might tear his garments for one of several reasons: to express remorse and repentance over the discovery of sin in his life or in the lives of his people; to protest in grief and sorrow a condition that violated God's Word; or to acknowledge personal unworthiness before the awesome manifestation of the holiness of God. Elisha's rending of his garment was a confession of his undoneness and inadequacy for the work to which he was called. But having done so, Elisha did not remain unclothed—he reached for the mantle of power by which he would show the world that the God of Elijah still lived. At the banks of the Jordan he touched the water with a sleeve of Elijah's mantle and cried, *"Where now is the Lord, the God of Elijah?"* Immediately the waters parted and Elisha crossed over. Elisha knew, as did the watching company of prophets from Jericho, that the power of the God of Elijah rested upon him.

Each of us will show how much we long for the Holy Spirit by the extent of our obedience to Christ. It is time for us to declare to the Lord that we shall not let Him go until He fills us with His Spirit. A mighty revival awaits those churches where a few leaders are willing to lead the way to the Upper Room for repentance and seeking God's face. We must desire His outpouring above all else, realizing that the swift waters of the Jordan will not part before a lesser power. The strongholds of evil cannot be destroyed by preaching alone. Those in bondage to greed and lust and pride and drugs cannot be delivered by human wisdom and love alone. Only God can do such mighty works of redemption, but He will work through those who are clothed in His power. Wesley Duewel wrote:

> There is always a tremendous difference between being a disciple of Christ indwelt by the Spirit, and being clothed with the Spirit, filled with the Spirit, and empowered with the Spirit. The Spirit must penetrate and possess all of our being. He must control us in all of His Lordship. He must pervade our personality. He must add a dimension of supernatural power.
>
> You dare not serve merely with a love for Christ. You must serve in the authority of Christ, with a personality consecrated to Christ. You must be infused with power from on high, suffused with the supernatural, imbued through and through with the holy, dynamic power of God...

But the one clothed with the power from on high, though still a dependent child of God, is enabled to live and serve in a new level of Spirit-given effectiveness. It is not the effectiveness of the person, but of God working through the person. It is the divine clothing, pervading, empowering the human as long as the person serves in total obedience to divine guidance, and in total appropriation of the divine provision.

The sacred mystery of divine empowering is that it is all of God in and through you, but it is always dependent on the obedient cooperation of your surrendered being.[4]

May we humbly enter the dressing room of preparation where God waits to fit us into His mantle of power.

# Notes

1. John R. W. Stott, *The Cross of Christ* (InterVarsity Press, 1986), p. 83.

2. Dietrich Bonnhoeffer, *The Cost of Discipleship* (Macmillan Pub. Co., 1961), pp. 46-47.

3. Lloyd Ogilvie, *Praying with Power* (Regal Books, 1983), *pp. 25-26*.

4. Wesley Duewel, *Ablaze for God* (Francis Asbury Press, 1989). pp. 44-46.

# Chapter 7

# Dead Churches Will Live Again

*The hand of the Lord was upon me, and he brought me out by the Spirit of the Lord and set me in the middle of a valley; it was full of bones. He led me back and forth among them, and I saw a great many bones on the floor of the valley, bones that were very dry. He asked me, "Son of man, can these bones live?"*

*I said, "O Sovereign Lord, you alone know."*

*Then he said to me, "Prophesy to these bones and say to them, 'Dry bones, hear the word of the Lord! This is what the Sovereign Lord says to these bones: I will make breath enter you, and you will come to life. Then you will know that I am the Lord.' "*

*So I prophesied as I was commanded. And as I was prophesying, there was a noise, a rattling sound, and the bones came together, bone to bone. I looked, and tendons and flesh appeared on them and skin covered them, but there was no breath in them.*

*Then he said to me, "Prophesy to the breath; prophesy, son of man, and say to it, 'This is what the Sovereign Lord says: Come from the four winds, O breath, and breathe into these slain, that they may live.' " So I prophesied as he commanded me, and breath entered them; they came to life and stood up on their feet—a vast army.*

Ezekiel 37:1-10

Ezekiel, a young temple priest in Jerusalem, was among those carried away into exile by Bayblonian King Nebuchadnezzar in 597 B.C. In that strange land he was called to be a prophet to the people of God in their captivity.

Ezekiel's message had a twofold purpose.

First, to interpret the times. With an embittered, depressed, self-pitying congregation that complained of suffering unjustly, the man of God had to come straight to the point: God's children cannot rebel against Him, defile their worship with idolatry and ignore the conditions of their covenant with Jehovah without tragic consequences. Babylon was God's sword of judgment on their unfaithfulness, and it was time for repentance.

Second, to inspire hope. Ezekiel began this task by destroying false hope. He attached self-appointed prophets who invented their own visions and messages by which to whitewash idolatry and rebellion. Ezekiel confronted both the false shepherds and their duped flocks by demanding a spirit of repentance and a sense of responsibility for their sad conditions. Only then could God's messenger promise a merciful outpouring of the Spirit of God that would mean renewal and restoration.

I pray that we shall not allow a sterile dispensationalism to rob us of Ezekiel's message of revival for God's people today. Whether or not we believe in a literal fulfillment of the promise to restore a Davidic dynasty to the nation of Israel in the last days, let us not forget that Ezekiel was a prophet of the New Covenant as well. All who come to God through faith in Christ, whether Jew or Gentile, are christened by the Holy Spirit as members of the new spiritual Israel, the Church. And in these last days, on the authority of the Word of our Sovereign God, He will again show forth the glory and power of His Son through His people as they come alive again in His Spirit. As multitudes repent and turn from the captivity of the world and the flesh, we shall see in the coming years the greatest revival in the history of the Church as God's people are restored to the fullness and freedom of the Spirit.

# A Valley of Bones

In his vision Ezekiel was led into a valley where long ago a mighty battle had left hundreds of thousands slain. No one had survived to bury the dead. Vultures had long since picked the carcasses clean, and there were the bones. The rains of the centuries had washed them thin, and a thousand summer suns had bleached them white as snow. It was a dismal scene.

## So Many and So Dry!

Like it or not, that valley of dry bones is a striking symbol of a lifeless church. The prophet did not miss a thing as the

Lord led him back and forth across the valley. "I saw a great many bones on the floor of the valley," he said *"bones that were very dry"* (emphasis added).

There are millions of dead Christians and thousands of dry churches scattered over the whole North American continent today. Several surveys support the following statistics representing those in the United States who are eighteen and older: 94% believe in God; 84% believe that Jesus Christ is the Son of God; 80% would like to see another great religious awakening; 77% believe there is a heaven; 58% believe there is a hell; 56% belong to a church; 32% attend church with some degree of regularity; 30% claim to have been born again or to have had a meaningful experience with Christ; 10% claim to be spiritually committed to the Christian faith.

The growth of the evangelical movement in this country since 1950 has been nothing short of phenomenal. Even if the report that nearly one in three adults is born again proves to be an exaggeration, it could still leave us with nearly fifty million professing evangelicals. That is a big pile of bones. The sad part of the story is that *most of us are very dry.*

## Great Form but No Power

A prominent Christian leader recently confided, "I doubt if over five percent of our evangelicals are living in the power of the Holy Spirit as Jesus promised in Acts 1:8." The apostle Paul warned that if we are not controlled by the Spirit, the alternative is to live according to the natural impulses—and this spells spiritual death (Rom. 8:1-14).

There's the dreadful smell of death on so much of the Church in these serious times. We may number in the millions, but the symptoms of death abound—we are too dead to hunger and thirst for the meat and milk of the Word, too life-less in our services to worship God freely and deeply in the Spirit, too insensitive to love one another and bear one another's burdens, too faithless and selfish to tithe, too powerless to prevail in prayer, too weak to witness for Jesus Christ.

Nothing can revive us now except the wind of the Spirit.

# A Vision of Revival

"Son of man, can these bones live?" the Lord asked Ezekiel. In other words, "Do you really believe that I can transform this appalling death valley into a garden of glory and life, Ezekiel?" The prophet was put to the test—did he, or did he not, believe in the God of the supernatural? This world is full of people who believe in the possible; men and women of God must believe in the impossible.

### "Own the Bones"

"Son of man, these bones are the whole house of Israel," God told the prophet. There was to be no misunderstanding the meaning of the vision. The people of God were like those bones—dead, drab, dull, boring, joyless, grim, defeated. Lloyd Ogilvie wrote:

The more I talk with contemporary church members and leaders over the country, the more I am convinced that the great need of American Christianity is for us to own the bones of dead institutionalism. All else has failed! We must admit, individually and corporately, our need for daily resurrection and the breath of the Holy Spirit to fill us!"[1]

But to own the bones is a blow to our carnal pride. Instead, too many pastors grow defensive and argue with the Laodicean leaders, "We are fine, we don't need a thing." Compounding their withered state is the element of deception—there are usually false signs of growth even among the dead and the dying. Organizational growth and numerical strength and financial ability are not the final proofs of spiritual life. A church can be strangely inspired by the spirit of this age to multiply its membership to raise more money to do impressive programs to build a great name for itself. Its only hope is to be stabbed awake by the words of a grieved Savior: "But you do not realize that you are wretched, pitiful, poor, blind and naked" (Rev. 3:17).

The Sardis church would not own the bones. It was too lifeless to discern between appearance and reality. "I know your reputation as a live and active church," the Lord told the congregation, *"but you are dead. Now wake up! Strengthen what little remains—for even what is left is at the point of death"* (Rev. 3:1-2, *TLB*, emphasis added).

Owning the bones is a preliminary stage of revival. But we do not do this until either a sudden or a growing awareness of our need shocks us, breaks us and drives us to repentance. Richard Owen Roberts described the kind of brokenness that brings revival:

> Conduct that has always seemed acceptable will appear unbelievably wicked. Prejudices that have characterized professing Christians for decades will be revealed for the grievous sins they really are. Private indulgences upon which a person has looked with favor for years will suddenly seem to merit all the wrath of God poured out forever. Prayerlessness, ignorance of Scripture, sins of omission, and failure in

good works will no longer be defended by a myriad of excuses, but will be laid open before the God "with whom we have to do."

Pride and self-centered living will no longer be excused as necessary defenses in a wicked world, but seen as the very essence of wickedness itself...agony over sin will be so great that the thought of prolonging life in the midst of such wickedness will be intolerable. From the very depths of men's beings will come the cry, "O God, save me from my self and sin, from my wickedness and depravity, or slay me; do not let me persist another day in this awful condition.[2]

Revival is God's only way of saving the Church from wicked selfishness. "If my people, who are called by my name," He challenges us, "will humble themselves and pray and seek my face and turn from their wicked ways, then will I hear from heaven and will forgive their sin and will heal their land" (II Chron. 7:14).

## Catch the Vision

God pressed the prophet, "Do you really believe I can bring these bones to life?" What could Ezekiel answer but, "O Sovereign Lord, you alone know if revival can come to this valley of dry bones." God wanted the prophet to completely identify with His passion to give revival. Only then could Ezekiel pray the divinely inspired prayer from the heart and declare with authority the coming revival to his dead congregation.

Christian leaders, please hear me. Long before the winds of the Spirit start to blow in our churches, even while our people have no ears to hear the voice of the Spirit, we must faithfully declare the Word of the Lord. Like Ezekiel, we must not stagger at His promise but we must say, "Dry bones, hear the word of the Sovereign Lord." No other message will bring revival.

Ezekiel was told to prophesy to the wind. This is tantamount to the New Testament believer prevailing with the Spirit of God, the Spirit of life, to breathe upon the paralyzed body of Christ and bring about the miracle of new life. This is done as we allow the Spirit to lead us back and forth and throughout the appalling condition of our dead churches until we are able to catch Christ's passion for reviving His people. We must catch His vision of a people with life. It becomes over a period of time a matter of allowing the Holy Spirit to pray Christ's prayer for revival through us. May God give us men and women in every church who will devote themselves to such praying!

Evangelist J. Wilbur Chapman told of preaching in Hereford, England, for several days without a single sign of the Spirit's moving. Then one day John Hyde came to town and visited the meeting. "When Praying Hyde came to town," said Chapman, "God came to town as well." Fifty people surrendered their hearts and lives to Christ on the night that the prayer warrior was in the service. Chapman begged Hyde to pray for him. They went into a room and Hyde locked the door. He turned his face up toward heaven and let the tears roll. Finally, he spoke just two words: "Oh, God!" Five minutes went by before he uttered another sound. Then all at once, the evangelist said, Hyde was talking to God out of the depths of his heart with such holy boldness that it was breathtaking. Chapman got a new filling of the Spirit that night, and the churches got a new Pentecost in the days that followed.

# A Visitation of the Spirit

As Ezekiel was prophesying to the bones, "there was a noise, a rattling sound, and the bones came together, bone to bone." Then tendons and skin covered the skeletons, and there they lay—a valley filled with forms without life. That a miracle had happened there was no denying. But Ezekiel had followed the Spirit and the Word of God too closely to mistake noise and appearance for real revival, even when there were miracles. The situation fell short of what God had promised. The prophet was not ready to announce success just because there was new movement in the church. He would not stop praying until divine life filled his dead congregation.

## A Mighty Revival

"So I prophesied as he commanded me," Ezekiel said, "and breath entered them; they came to life and stood up on their feet—a vast army." Here at last was what God had promised and what the prophet had prayed for—a people alive in the Spirit, filled with love and joy, and liberated for worship and praise and empowered to witness to the startled nations.

Some are pointing to the three unusual movements in this country during the twentieth century (the rise of Pentecostalism in the early 1900s, the Charismatic renewal beginning in the 1950s, and the phenomenal growth among evangelicals since World War II) as the closest we can expect to come to the great historic awakenings. There is no denying that God has used these three movements in remarkable ways, for the blessings from each of them would fill volumes. But with Lewis Drummond, we have to ask:

What has happened to the overwhelming majority of God's people? Why hasn't the mainstream of the church been moved?[3]

The sad truth is that the bulk of the bones has gone untouched and unraised as yet. This is seen in the the number of evils that must be dealt with in praying for revival.

● *Deadness*—There are exceptions, but in most congregations only a few are alive in the Spirit and ready to celebrate the glorious Being of God in praise and worship. The majority wants only good organization, sound doctrine, orderly services, enlighted speakers, and to personally be let alone.

● *Division*—The way Charismatics and non-Charismatics treat each other—often completely ignoring one another—makes a travesty of the unity of believers that Christ prayed for. The attitudes and remarks that pass between Calvinists and Arminians must sorely grieve the Holy Spirit.

● *Little or No Passion for Holiness*—When most do not hunger and thirst for righteousness and true holiness, their emptiness assures their seduction by the god of this age.

● *The Troubled Home*—So often the Christian home is compromised by the same elements making up the worldly home—disorder, rebellion, materialism, unfaithfulness and resentment.

● *Prayerlessness*—Only a tiny remnant claims to have a definite commitment to a meaningful prayer ministry.

● *Independence*—Church members do not want to make commitments to responsible ministries. They will not be tied down in a way that prevents their frequent weekend holidays. They dream and speak of freedom, while falling deeper into bondage.

● *Ignorance of Spiritual Warfare*—Richard Lovelace said:

> Although part of the church pays lip service to the reality of sin and worldliness and even demonic agents, it seems to me that much of the church's warfare today is fought by blindfolded soldiers who cannot see the forces ranged against them, who are buffeted by invisible opponents and respond by striking one another.

> Only a mighty revival of historic magnitude can purge these horrible diseases from the body of Christ. It must not be forgotten that revival begins with the household of God, and then it spreads to the world that is lost.[4]

Revival is the Wind of the Spirit breathing new life and power into the paralyzed body of Christ.

Revival is the Waters of the Spirit breaking forth on the Church in abundance—downpouring, infilling, outflowing.

Revival is the Oil of the Spirit flowing forth to heal our diseased hearts, refill our flickering lamps and anoint our weak souls.

Revival is the Dove of the Spirit descending with peace and purity upon anguished minds and divided hearts.

Revival is the Mantle of the Spirit clothing the Church with Christ's power to live and love and witness to a needy world.

## A Militant Force

Ezekiel witnessed the mighty miracle of a valley full of dry bones being transformed into a great army. "They came to life," he said, "and stood up on their feet—a vast army."

The revived Church is a militant one. Satanic hordes shiver and retreat before its waving banners and drawn swords. With hearts on fire and wearing the full armor of God, Spirit-led soldiers act on the amazing authority of their risen Lord and order the destruction of the strongholds of evil. Principalities and powers of the world of darkness yield, and the doors of the Kingdom of God are opened to receive multitudes of hungry souls held in captivity.

Here in America we have the talented church, the organized church, the educated church, the financed church, the equipped church. But nothing will count unless we have *the revived Church.*

Not since the middle of the nineteenth century has America heard the full roar of Pentecost blowing through her churches. But God is even now leading some of His anointed men and women on an inspection tour of the American valley of dry bones. As they walk with Him over the lengths and depths of the appalling spiritual conditions, He is sharing with them His purpose for a great awakening. As He gives them a revelation of what is to come, their sighs of depression turn into sobs of intercession. Their small but growing number will soon form the critical mass for the greatest spiritual explosion in the history of the Church.

Let us pray: *O God, wake us up to hear Your call to the Upper Room. Give us a new vision of Your mighty fullness so that we can cry for cleansing and tarry for power. May your Spirit then flow unhindered through our believing, burning hearts in true intercession for a dead Church and a lost world. Baptize us with a bold faith to declare to both worlds that You are about to pour out Your Spirit on Your People in measures never known before. O God, may we not waver, but keep on praying until revival comes.*

## Notes

1. Lloyd Ogilvie, *Lord of the Impossible* (Abingdon Press, 1984), p. 218.

2. Richard Owen Roberts, *Revival!* (Tyndale House, 1983), pp. 23-24.

3. Lewis A. Drummond, *The Awakening that Must Come* (Broadman Press, 1978), p. 31.

4. Richard F. Lovelace, *Dynamics of Spiritual Life* (InterVarsity, 1980), p. 18.

# CHRISTIAN ◆◆ RENEWAL

*A Journal on Prayer, Revival, and the Spirit-filled Life*

| Vol. 5, No. 3 | An Evangelical Quarterly | Summer, 1990 |

# A MIGHTY MINORITY

*I ask then, Did God reject his people? By no means! I am an Israelite myself, a descendant of Abraham, from the tribe of Benjamin. God did not reject his people, whom he foreknew. Don't you know what the Scripture says in the passage About Elijah -- how he appealed to God against*

James W. Tharp

*Israel: "Lord, they have killed your prophets and torn down your altars; I am the only one left, and they are trying to kill me"? And what was God's answer to him? "I have reserved for myself seven thousand who have not bowed the knee to Baal." So too, at the present time there is a remnant chosen by grace.*

*(Romans 11: 1-5)*

Many people, including believers and nonbelievers, believe that the sun is setting on Western Civilization. Who can deny that deepening shadows are falling across our religious freedoms, our sacred values of family life and the socio-economic infrastructure here in what was once God-fearing America?

This writer sincerely believes that we are living in that late hour of human history in which God declared that He would shake the heavens and the earth, and that such a judgment would extend to all nations (Haggai 2: 6-7; Heb. 12: 25-29). But He does not leave us in the dark as to His purpose for such sweeping judgment -- to establish His unshakable kingdom through His Son, Jesus Christ.

Let us not think that the church will escape the wrath of God. His own people have distorted and defiled the Gospel and betrayed their Lord. Even now her lampstand is being removed and her house is becoming desolate.

# The School of Prayer

Since 1986, thousands of Christians have experienced a transformation of their prayer lives in response to this six-hour seminar with James W. Tharp. The course is divided in three sections: (1) *A Theology of Prayer*; (2) *An Authority in Prayer*; and (3) *A Strategy for Prayer*.

Pastors and Christian leaders who are interested in bringing the School of Prayer Seminar to their church or city may write for a free brochure to: *Christian Renewal*, 5595 Love Lane, Bozeman, Montana 59715.

*The School of Prayer on Audio Cassette*—All six hours of Biblical exposition is on tape, and it can be yours for a contribution of only $20.00 to *Christian Renewal*. This also includes the workbook. Order your album now.